University of Plymouth
Charles Seale Hayne Library
Subject to status this item may be renewed
via your Primo account

http://primo.plymouth.ac.uk
Tel: (01752) 588588

The Sociology of Disability and Inclusive Education

Len Barton's intellectual and practical contribution to the sociology of disability and education is highly significant and widely known. The leading scholars in this collection, including his long term collaborators, offer both a celebration and a reassessment of this contribution, addressing the challenge that the social model of disability has presented to dominant medicalised concepts, categories and practices, and their power to define the identity and the lives of others. At the same time the authors build upon some of the key themes that are woven through Len Barton's work, such as his call for a 'politics of hope'.

This collection explores a wide range of topics, including:

- difference as a field of political struggle
- the relationship of disability studies, disabled people and their struggle for inclusion
- radical activism: organic intellectuals and the disability movement
- discrimination, exclusion and effective change
- inclusive education
- the 'politics of hope', resilience and transformative actions
- universal pedagogy, human rights and citizenship debates.

The Sociology of Disability and Inclusive Education highlights Len Barton's humane vision of academic work, of the nature of an inclusive and non-discriminatory society, of the role of an education system which addresses the rights, and potential of all participants. It indicates how such a society could be achieved through the principles of social inclusion, human rights, equity and social justice.

This book was originally published as a special issue of *British Journal of Sociology of Education.*

Madeleine Arnot is Professor of Sociology of Education at Cambridge University, UK, and Professorial Fellow at Jesus College. She is a Fellow of the Academy of Social Sciences and Chair of the Executive Editorial Board of the British Journal of Sociology of Education. Recent publications include *Education, Asylum and the 'Non-citizen' child: The politics of compassion and belonging* (2010, with H. Pinson and M. Candappa); *Educating the Gendered Citizen: sociological engagements with national and global agendas* (2009); and *Gender Education and Equality in a Global Context* (2008, ed. with S. Fennell).

First published 2012
by Routledge
2 Park Square, Milton Park, Abingdon, Oxon, OX14 4RN

Simultaneously published in the USA and Canada
by Routledge
711 Third Avenue, New York, NY 10017

Routledge is an imprint of the Taylor & Francis Group, an informa business

This book is a reproduction of the *British Journal of Sociology of Education*, volume 31, issue 5. The Publisher requests to those authors who may be citing this book to state, also, the bibliographical details of the special issue on which the book was based.

Trademark notice: Product or corporate names may be trademarks or registered trademarks, and are used only for identification and explanation without intent to infringe.

British Library Cataloguing in Publication Data
A catalogue record for this book is available from the British Library

ISBN13: 978-0-415-69353-0

Typeset in Times New Roman
by Taylor & Francis Books

Publisher's Note
The publisher would like to make readers aware that the chapters in this book may be referred to as articles as they are identical to the articles published in the special issue. The publisher accepts responsibility for any inconsistencies that may have arisen in the course of preparing this volume for print.

The Sociology of Disability and Inclusive Education

A Tribute to Len Barton

Edited by
Madeleine Arnot

Routledge
Taylor & Francis Group

LONDON AND NEW YORK

Contents

Framing the sociology of disability and inclusive education: an introduction

In September 2009, Len Barton retired as Chair of the Executive Editorial Board of the *British Journal of Sociology of Education* (BJSE). Past and present members of the Executive and Editorial Boards and the international consultants owe a great debt of gratitude to Len. He was not only the founding editor and first Chair but also a superb friend and colleague who has closely worked with us over the past 30 years. There is hardly a sociologist of education internationally and in the United Kingdom who has not come across Len Barton and his extraordinary pivotal role in the discipline. In tribute to him, the Executive Editorial Board ran a major celebratory event to thank Len for the part that he has played in promoting critical, analytic and informed sociological studies of education, and his unique contribution in establishing and running BJSE and consolidating its world-class status as *the* sociology of education journal. The Board also decided to publish a special issue of the journal on *The Sociology of Disability and Education* as a tribute to Len's lifelong commitment to the development of this field of study and in recognition of the exceptional leadership and scholarship he has offered to sociological studies of disability and inclusive education.

In 1978, whilst many of us were happily dancing to 'The YMCA' at the legendary Annual Sociology of Education Conference, which started at Westhill College, Birmingham and continued at different locations for over two decades, Len was busy talking to a wide group of people about the idea of a journal[1] in the sociology of education. The first Executive Board was set up with seven members – Len, Olive Banks, Roger Dale, David Hargreaves, Roland Meighan, Ivan Reid and Graham Vulliamy, along with Roger Osborn King from Carfax Publishing. They began to establish the policy and direction of the journal and helped identify and confirm the members of the first editorial board[2] – some of whom are still on board today. Little did we know that we would still be working on the journal 30 years later! One of the great tributes to Len's editorial leadership of the BJSE is the extraordinary continuity of editors who have remained working on this journal and the fact that some 88 sociologists of education, now leading figures in the social analysis of education and education policy globally, have been associated with the journal as editors. As Chair of the Executive Board, Len created a culture that held sacrosanct the concept of sociology as a critical discipline that could delve behind taken for granted assumptions about social reality and mythological policy discourses, revealing the social and political nature of education. The contribution of the journal would be to stand outside mainstream educational thinking and offer critical but also constructive and innovative insights into the shaping by social structures of the processes of teaching, learning, educational choices and achievements At the core of Len's sociological project, as so many contributors to this special issue point out, was C. Wright Mills' (1959) concept of the 'sociological imagination' strongly framed by notions of professional and political integrity.

Over the 30 years of his stewardship, Len practised what he preached. To the sociology of education he brought the discipline of a person committed to principled professionalism. His relationship with editors, authors, reviewers and publishers epitomised the highest standards of honesty and complete commitment to the quality of the project. Because of this professionalism and the humane culture that Len represented, the BJSE has managed to survive, adapt and grow across a period in which the field itself and our research as sociologists has repeatedly been buffeted by political scepticism about its value. We only have to think back to the New Right challenges in the early 1980s, which claimed that sociology of education was an 'unnecessary, costly and harmful ideology', characterised by 'political bias, subversion, irrelevance and weak scholarship' (Dawson 1981, 60) – something that should be cut out of training courses for teachers in order to improve 'the moral environment' in which teachers are trained (Cox and Marks 1982 quoted in Arnot and Barton 1992).

In 1980, the first volume of BJSE represented a symbolic turning point for our discipline. Sociology of education *came of age* at that key moment. BJSE became the first genuinely international journal of sociology of education, even if British based. Its stated goal was to attract sociological analysts internationally (we did not use the global word then). The first editorial argued that the journal would prove that the field could sustain its own journal – that it was a genuine field in its own right. The journal never promised or assumed a consensus since it expected to promote a diversity of theoretical and methodological approaches. Editors, as referees, recognise the need to allow new theoretical paradigms and new voices to come through and the need for the journal to grow with the times and to provide the necessary space within which to engage with major educational reforms. As the journal has moved through the eras of social democratic consensus in education (in the United Kingdom at least), contributors have recounted the growing complexities of globalisation for the modern educational project – they consider, in considerable depth, the political implications of neo-liberalism for the teaching profession, for the changing nature of pedagogy, curriculum and evaluation, and for the shaping of young people's lives and the social order generally.

The space that Len held open for our discipline therefore houses a unique combination of stability and continuity as well as a political dynamic in which social theory of education can grow independently of external interference. That space is never quiet – the journal has created and hosted intellectual dialogues about the changing nature of society and its educational systems. In the period marked by Len Barton's editorial leadership, international conversations were held about the values of phenomenology, classroom interaction, social reproduction theory and political economy; it has demonstrated the ongoing significance of, for example, Marxist and neo-Marxist, Weberian and Durkheimian theories of conflict, status and knowledge, the power of Bourdieudian and Bernsteinian theorising, and Foucauldian, feminist and Butlerian analyses of discourse, regulation and subjectivities. Studies of youth cultures, globalised media cultures, school cultures, gender cultures and minority ethnic cultures have fed into sociological debates about the universalism and relativism of knowledge, multicultural, cosmopolitan and now global curricula and their power to address social inequalities embedded in patterns of choice, performance and livelihoods. Sociological studies published in the BJSE range from the youngest child's experience in an infant school through to an analysis of their progress in and out of state and private educational institutions into tertiary, adult and vocational education. In 2006, when the Executive Editorial Board published some of the seminal BJSE articles in an edited collection *Education in Society* (Barton 2007), we confirmed for ourselves just how much we had sustained the original project – to publish independent, high quality analyses of how educational processes, institutions and systems were not only embedded within 'the social' but how they constructed, reproduced, produced and regulated 'the social'.

The BJSE has at its heart a commitment to *social justice* and *social progress.* Throughout Len's leadership, despite the economic and political turmoil of the late-twentieth century and early-twenty-first century, sociology of education has continued to address the political imperatives of social justice. The purposes of research and its professional ethics and ethos are thus so defined. This special issue captures Len's own engagement with such political/moral ambitions. As all of the authors in this special issue testify, the intellectual project with which Len's work and reputation are associated is one of engaging with the inequalities found in society, whether they are inequalities experienced by the working class, the disabled, women, marginalised ethnic and religious groups, gay and lesbian groups, migrants or just the young. His political mission, which was so clearly expressed in relation to those defined by society as 'disabled', was shaped by his deep understanding of the purposes of sociological scholarship.

Len's contribution to the sociology of disability and inclusive education internationally therefore symbolises a particular political stance on the importance and social relevance of the production of new knowledge and the quest for more understanding of what was needed intellectually in terms of engagements with governments, communities, specific groups in society and social movements.

This collection comes directly out of that culture and that experience. By publishing this book, the Executive Editorial Board of the BJSE wanted to acknowledge the role that Len has played in relation to the development of the sociology of education and disability and to identify the ongoing contemporary debates. Len Barton's own scholarship in the field of disability, as the authors demonstrate, is as remarkable. His academic research, writing and lecturing helped define the ground rules for a new subfield of the sociology of disability and inclusive education. His active engagement with the disability movement, his framing with colleagues of the sociological and political analysis of disability, his challenge to educationalists and educational policy-makers in the United Kingdom and in many other countries has been exceptional.

A sociology of disability and inclusive education

Len's intellectual mission was not only to define the parameters of the sociology of disability, but also to work with others to move it forward into new conceptualisations of social inclusion and inclusive education. In a BJSE review of *Policy, Experience and Change: Cross Cultural Reflections on Inclusive Education* (Barton and Armstrong 2007), which Len co-edited with Felicity Armstrong, Alan Roulstone (2008) points to the tension that they reveal between *homo economicus* promoted through neo-liberal governmental policies and the broader notion of *homo humanus* which the editors wished to promote. The goals here are not those of 'piecemeal steps' and reformist politics with discursive tokenism towards inclusive education, but a major change in values, a new humanised education system and humane vision of what can be achieved through the principles of inclusion. Roulstone quotes from Barton and Armstrong's book:

> For us inclusive education is not an end in itself, but a means to an end. It is about contributing to the realisation of an inclusive society with a demand for a rights approach as a central component of policy-making. Thus the question is fundamentally about issues of human rights, equity, social justice and the struggle for a non-discriminatory society. These principles are at the heart of inclusive educational policy and practice. (Barton and Armstrong 2007, 6)

This approach to the subfield of sociology of disability and education, which involves identifying the problematics and political yardsticks with which to assess governments' policies, is well described by the contributors to this collection of tributes. Len's contribution has been to work collaboratively and actively to radicalise the academic and policy terrain by mainstreaming the lives, identities and politics of those with disabilities into critical educational debates. Central to his sociological project therefore has been a forceful, challenging engagement with the realities of *difference as a field of political struggle*. As Sally Tomlinson recounts and Mike Oliver and Colin Barnes demonstrate in their contributions, the sociology of disability shifted pathological often medical discourses and their pedagogies around special needs, handicap, behaviour problems and mental retardation towards the so-called 'social model of disability'. At the heart of this model is the recognition of the power of some to define the identity and lives of others; tragically such power creates disempowerment, marginalisation and dependency especially for those with disabilities (Barton 1993). Len's project has been to encourage other social theorists to recognise that the demands of society are no more heavily felt than by those who are 'read', classified, surveilled and institutionalised as 'disabled' (Barton 1993). Disability therefore is about 'social restriction' through 'the politics of definition'.

In his inaugural speech (Barton 1993), Len argued that academics should recognise the ways in which all 'oppressed and discriminated people struggle to develop a sense of self worth and resistance based on an alternative set of values and interpretations'. As the contributions of Len's close colleagues Mike Oliver and Colin Barnes indicate, what gives strength and uniqueness to the sociology of disability and education is the close association established between disability studies, disabled people and their struggle for inclusion. Yet as they point out, whilst there are some positive signs in the take up of the social model of disability, there is still limited progress in terms of developing the sort of principles of inclusion required. The relationship between academic and activist work is emphasised by Kathleen Lynch, who brings to the fore the powerful significance of Len Barton's understanding of universities as sites of the Gramscian-styled activism of an organic intellectual *for* and *on behalf of* social movements (such as those with disabilities) and the urgency of developing universities as public interest institutions. The emphasis on voice is also central to Len's work, as Roger Slee points out, which is connected to the genuine humility in Len's own understanding of his relationship with the disability movement. Within this context, Len's sociological analysis of disability, as Susan Peters' article leads us to understand, offers a 'politics of hope' in which the voices of those who are disabled, if listened to, can bring transformation, and make public forms of personal and collective resilience.

What these contributors offer are insights into where the field of sociology of disability and education needs to develop. The contributions by Julie Allan, on the one hand, and by Marcia Rioux and Paulo Pinto on the other, point to some of the ways forward. Allen stresses the value of now re-engaging with disability politics and taking more responsibility for the 'Other' by 'refusing to reduce inclusive education to what Len called 'quick slick responses' by governments. Marcia Rioux and Paulo Pinto emphasise the value of engaging in critical discussions of the concepts of universal pedagogy, human rights and concerns about autonomy and dignity. The relationship of disability to the development world opens the door to these new citizenship debates.

In his reply in this volume, Len reflects on his own contribution to the field of disability and inclusive education. With usual modesty, he recognises the centrality of 'solidarity, critical friendships and supportive networks' that characterise his own experience of the academy and working outside of it. Disability Studies has moved from being a 'single issue factor' to one where it can be embedded within human rights based policy and practice. The politicisation of disability emerged through the development initially of a social model of disability that rejected pathological medicalised models of disability, however as Len acknowledges, for some, this new model did not go far enough. The social model of disability has had to go beyond the issue of disablement connecting with other forms of discrimination. The political analysis he encourages is one which links disability and inclusion to globalisation and the inequalities associated with disability, poverty and the new vulnerabilities associated with global political economies. In this context, a sociological analysis of disability is needed that addresses, for example: political strategic thinking around critical friendships, humility, respect for disabled people and their voicing of concerns, and participatory citizenship. 'The politics of hope' that is associated with this agenda is as optimistic as it is serious about the power of research when linked to an egalitarian politics.

In colleagueship

The agenda which Len Barton established as part of the sociology of disability and inclusion was one which he daily practices in his own participation in higher education. He is the first to argue that sociologists (like others in this particular institutional setting) should uncover discriminatory practices whether through research or through a personal engagement with the institutions within which we work. Because of his awareness of the structures and processes of discrimination and injustice generally, he has been able personally and professionally to support colleagues working in critical social class studies, gender equality, race and ethnic studies and other social justice fields. As a colleague, he is noted for being keenly aware of the conditions under which we work and hope to succeed. His support for sociological colleagues nationally and internationally is legendary. The BJSE gave him extensive knowledge about where and when sociologists were struggling to find a voice and he employed such knowledge to offer assistance and advice. Using the journal as a platform, he applied his knowledge to nurture so many careers, to support our writing, to encourage us to speak at his conferences, to help with applications for jobs and promotion. He has been a quite extraordinary friend to us all. The long list of his edited collections in sociology of education[3] and the sociological conferences[4] he ran over the same period demonstrate his commitment to promote young academics, to network scholars across borders, boundaries and hierarchies, to disseminate widely sociological studies of education and most importantly, to keep the field moving forward into new terrains.

In commissioning and collating these original papers by leading writers in the field of sociology of disability and education, the Executive Editorial Board of the BJSE were clear that the aim was to record and recognise Len's own scholarly contribution to the sociology of disability and education and the directions it is now taking. But it was also, as is evident, to thank Len for his role within the journal. Basil Bernstein once infamously described the BJSE as 'Len's journal'. And, of course, it *is* Len's journal. He was a brilliant Chair of the Executive Editorial Board. He viewed articles as one might original paintings, always representative of a creative act; he viewed peer reviewers' reports as 'gifts' for which authors needed to be grateful, not least for the time and energy expended on their behalf; he promoted the journal as a major collective enterprise in which all had contributed. Great was his appreciation of, and friendship with, the two journal secretaries: Val Stokes and Helen Oliver. In all matters to do with the journal he demonstrated the value of a strong professional ethic and intellectual independence from the ever increasing demands of commercialism. He remains a passionate advocate for the value of a person's opinion and the need to work with difference rather than constrain or silence it. In that sense, he defines the morality and scholarly standards in academic publishing.

Finally, through this collection, as Executive Editors, we want collectively to thank Len for his 'other side' – a side that the Executive Board has been privileged enough to see. He is probably the only journal editor who took his Executive Board on busman's holidays around the country. He specialised in the away-day as the means of creating the right environment for colleagueship. Boat trips in Scarborough, visits to Brighton pier, shopping in Harrogate, rides on the big dipper and dodgem cars in Blackpool, the site of Len's childhood – these are fond memories for which we are enormously grateful. The purpose of such trips was initially to work on special issues of the journal. Latterly they were to consolidate the future of the journal, its identity and its support for the future development of sociology of education. For these, he needs to be reassured.

Madeleine Arnot - *Faculty of Education, University of Cambridge, UK*
Philip Brown - *School of Social Sciences, Cardiff University, UK*
Amanda Coffey - *School of Social Sciences, Cardiff University, UK*
Miriam David - *Institute of Education, University of London, UK*
Lynn Davies - *School of Education University of Birmingham, UK*
David James – *School of Social Sciences, Cardiff University, UK*
Rajani Naidoo - *School of Management, University of Bath, UK*
Diane Reay - *Faculty of Education, University of Cambridge, UK*
Ivan Reid - *School of Lifelong Education, University of Bradford, UK*
Carol Vincent - *Institute of Education, University of London, UK*

Members of the Executive Editorial Board of the British Journal of Sociology of Education

Acknowledgements

We would like to thank Helen Oliver for her help in bringing this project to fruition and Mary Fuller for her assistance in reviewing papers.

Notes

1 Ivan Reid, in his paper 'Past and Present Trends in the Sociology of Education' presented at the 1977 Westhill conference, noted 'there was not even a British journal for the subject'.
2 M. Archer, G. Bernbaum, B. Bernstein, M. David, B. Davies, L. Davies, S. Delamont, T. Edwards, J. Eggleston, R. Johnson, M. MacDonald (now Arnot), A. McPherson, D. Reynold, W. Taylor, G. Whitty, B.Williamson and M. Young, with M. Apple, Z. Ferge, P. Musgrave and D. Smith as overseas consultants.
3 See references for a list of Len Barton's major publications.
4 Originally the Westhill Conference of Sociology of Education held in Birmingham every January from 1976 to 1992 and latterly the International Sociology of Education Conference held since 1993, first in Sheffield and then in London.

References

Arnot, M., and L. Barton, eds. 1992. *Voicing concerns: Sociological perspectives on contemporary education reforms.* Oxford: Symposium Books.

Barton, L. 1993. *Inaugural lecture,* University of Sheffield, November 17. http:// www.leeds.ac.uk/ disability- studies/archiveuk/barton/inaugral%20lecture%20barton.pdf (accessed June 1, 2010).

Barton, L. ed. 2007. *Education in society: 25 years of the British Journal of Sociology of Education,* London: Routledge.

Cox, C., and J. Marks. 1982. 'What has Athens to do with Jerusalem? Teaching sociology to students on medical, nursing, education and science courses'. In *The right to learn: Purpose, professionalism and account ability in state education,* ed. C. Cox and J. Marks. London: Centre for Policy Studies.

Dawson, G. 1981. 'Unfitting teachers to teach: Sociology in the training of teachers'. In *The pied pipers of education,* ed. D. Anderson. London: Social Affairs Unit.

Mills, C.W. 1959. *The sociological imagination.* London: Oxford University Press.

Roulstone, A. 2008. 'Extended review of Barton and Armstrong'. *British Journal of Sociology of Education* 29, no. 1: 113–16.

Len Barton's major publications

Barton, L and Meighan, R. eds. 1978. *Sociological interpretations of schooling and classrooms: A reappraisal*. Driffield: Nafferton Books.

Barton, L. and Meighan, R. eds. 1979. *Schools, pupils and deviance*. Driffield: Nafferton Books.

Barton, L.and Walker, S. and Meighan, R. eds. 1980. *Schooling, ideology and the curriculum*. Lewes: Falmer Press.

Barton, L. and Walker, S. eds. 1981. *Schools, teachers and teaching*. Lewes: Falmer Press.

Barton, L. and Walker, S. 1981. Four chapters on sociological perspectives in Meighan, R. *A sociology of educating*. London: Cassell.

Lawn, M. and Barton, L. eds. 1981. *Rethinking curriculum studies*. Beckenham: Croom Helm.

Barton, L. and Tomlinson, S. ed. 1981. *Special education: Policy, practices and social issues*. London: Harper Row.

Barton, L. and Walker. S. eds. 1983. *Race, class and education*. Beckenham: Croom Helm.

Walker, S. and Barton, L. eds. 1983. *Gender, class and education*. Lewes: Falmer Press.

Barton, L. and Walker, S. eds. 1984. *Social crisis and educational research*. Beckenham: Croom Helm.

Barton, L. and Tomlinson, S. eds. 1984. *Special education and social interests*. Beckenham: Croom Helm.

Barton, L. and Walker, S. eds. 1985. *Education and social change*. Beckenham: Croom Helm.

Walker,S. and Barton, L. eds. 1986. *Youth unemployment and schooling*. Milton Keynes: Open University Press.

Walker, S. and Barton, L. eds. 1987. *Changing policies, changing teachers*. Lewes: Falmer Press.

Barton, L. ed. 1988. *The politics of special educational needs*. Lewes: Falmer Press.

Walker, S. and Barton, L. eds. 1989. *Politics and processes of schooling*. Milton Keynes: Open University Press.

Barton, L. ed. 1989. *Disability and dependency*. Lewes: Falmer Press.

Barton, L. ed. 1989. *Integration, myth or reality?* Lewes: Falmer Press.

Arnot, M. and Barton, L. eds. 1992. *Voicing concerns: Sociological perspectives on contemporary education reforms*. Oxford: Symposium Books.

Corbett, J. and Barton, L. 1992. *Struggle for choice: Students with special needs in transition to adulthood*. London: Routledge.

Corbett, J. and Barton, L. 1992. *Facing challenges: The changing perspectives of special needs co-ordinators*. London: Skill. National Bureau for Students with Disabilities.

Clough, P. and Barton, L. eds. 1995. *Making difficulties: Research and construction of special educational needs*. London: Paul Chapman.

Barton, L. ed. 1996. *Disability and society. Emerging issues and insights*. London: Paul Chapman

Barton, L and Oliver, M. eds. 1997. *Disability studies, past, present and future*. Leeds: Leeds Disability Press.

Clough, P. and Barton, L. eds. 1998. *Articulating with difficulty: Research voices in inclusive education.* London: Paul Chapman.

Armstrong, F., Armstrong, D. and Barton, L. eds. 1999 *Inclusive education: Policy, contexts and comparative perspectives.* London: Fulton Books.

Armstrong, F., Armstrong, D. and Barton, L. eds. 1999. *Disability, human rights and education: Cross-cultural perspectives.* Buckingham: Open University Press.

Armstrong, F. and Barton, L. eds. 1999. *Difference and difficulty: Insights, issues and dilemmas.* Sheffield: Department of Educational Studies.

Furlong, J., Barton, L., Miles, S., Whiting, C. and Whitty, C. 2000. *Teacher education in transition. Re-forming professionalism?* Buckingham: Open University Press.

Barton, L. ed. 2001. *Disability, politics and the struggle for change.* London: David Fulton.

Barnes, C. Barton, L. and Oliver, M. eds. 2002. *Disability studies today,* Cambridge: Polity Press.

Barton, L. 2003. *Inclusive education and teacher education.* London University: Institute of Education Publication.

Barton, L. ed. 2006. *Overcoming disabling barriers: 18 years of disability and society.* London: Routledge.

Barton, L., ed. 2007. *Society and education: 25 years of British Journal of Sociology of Education.* London: Routledge.

Barton, L., and Armstrong, F. eds. 2007. *Policy, experience and change: Cross- cultural reflections on inclusive education.* Dordrecht: Springer.

Related Book Series

Len Barton has been the editor of successful Book Series with the following publishers: Croom Helm; Falmer Press and Open University Press. He also was co-editor for a Book Series with Springer Books.

Journals

Len was the founder and editor of the following International journals: *British Journal of Sociology of Education*; *International Studies in Sociology of Education*; *Disability and Society* and *Teaching in Higher Education.*

A tribute to Len Barton

Sally Tomlinson

Department of Education, University of Oxford, Oxford, UK

This article constitutes a short personal tribute to Len Barton in honour of his work and our collegial relationship going back over 30 years. It covers how Len saw his intellectual project of providing critical sociological and political perspectives on special education, disability and inclusion, and his own radical political perspectives. Len's challenges to prevailing notions of individual deficiencies of intellect, and disability as a personal misfortune, are noted, as is his profound influence on practitioners, activists, students and academics worldwide. It concludes that his goal of challenging and unsettling conventional 'ways of knowing' has had wide and lasting influence and that it is imperative to understand what moral, economic and political judgements lie behind decisions to separate, segregate and exclude young people from mainstream education and their fellow citizens.

Introduction

The chances of a carpenter becoming a university professor must be reasonably rare in Britain, a country dominated, despite talk of social mobility, by elites who still believe that the manual working class should gratefully prop up the social class hierarchy. However, this was the starting point for Len Barton. Brought up with his brother by a single-parent mother in the north of England, and attending a secondary modern school where he later noted he was labelled as ' unintelligent and thick', he left to serve an apprenticeship as a joiner. He eventually qualified as a teacher of what were then described as the 'mentally handicapped', teaching woodwork and swimming. In 1976 Len was appointed to a lectureship at Westhill College of Higher Education in Birmingham, which was where I met him in 1977. At that time I was researching the issue of the over-representation of black and working-class children in schools for what were then known as the 'educationally subnormal' in Birmingham. It was a joy to meet a colleague who shared my view that there was a pressing need to acquire wider social, historical, political and economic perspectives on the policies and practices that made up the sub-section of the education system known as special education. Our shared interests quickly resulted in two edited books (Barton and Tomlinson 1981, 1984) and what is to date 32 years of friendship. While not wishing to write a hagiography, over the years my admiration for Len and his achievements has increased exponentially. His own academic work, while continually offering a critical perspective on accepted practices and the ideologies of the powerful, has been imbued with a passion for social justice and an end to discrimination of any sort. He has communicated this passion for 'challenging and unsettling conventional ways of knowing' (Allen and Slee 2008, 87) in his teaching at all levels over the years, he has encouraged and assisted numerous attendees and writers at the conferences he has organised and through the journals he has edited, and his influence on disability studies and support for the disability movement has been immense. Many of his doctoral students are now employed at universities in Europe and around the world.

It was at Westhill College that Len first organised the Annual Sociology of Education Conferences and founded the *British Journal of Sociology of Education*, becoming its Chair of Editors until June 2009. In 1985 he left for Bristol Polytechnic (later the University of the West of England), where he was given a Professorship and served as Head of Professional Development. In 1990 he moved to a Chair at Sheffield University, taking over as Head of Department of Education and Developing an Inclusive Education Research Centre. His was the first Department in the country to teach an MEd in Inclusive Education. From 2000 to 2004 Len was Professor of Inclusive Education and Dean of Professional Development at the Institute of Education, London University – on retirement becoming an Emeritus Professor and continuing to research, and to teach in the United Kingdom and other countries. In 1986 Len founded and became the editor of the international journal devoted solely to disability issues. This was *Disability, Handicap and Society*, renamed *Disability and Society* in 1993. He also founded and developed the journals *Teaching in Higher Education* and *International Studies in the Sociology of Education*. He edited/co edited four book series, for Croom Helm, Taylor and Francis, the Open University Press, and Springer Books. The books in these series cover special educational needs, inclusive education, equity in education, disability and human rights, and Len encouraged authors concerned with developing conceptual, empirical and theoretical perspectives in these areas. I am not sure when Len took to wearing what became his trademark wide-brimmed fedora hat, but it marked him out as a familiar figure in all venues – although when I took him to the bar in the University Club at Oxford, after he had examined a doctorate, the barman enquired whether he was Harry Secombe![1]

Critical perspectives

Although it is not easy to select from the extensive number of written, edited and co-edited volumes, chapters, articles and papers produced over the years,

Len's intellectual journey over the past 35 years has followed a trajectory of critiques of special education, support for the disability movement, and critical analysis of moves in schools and society towards integration and inclusion. His analysis and influence on understandings of inclusion and inclusive practices continues to be crucially important (Barton 1997). By the end of the 1970s Len was clear that sociological and political perspectives on special education and special educational needs – the term popularised by the Warnock Report (DES 1978) – were necessary to make clear what moral and political judgements lay behind policies and practices in special education. In Britain, as in the USA and Australia particularly, there was anxiety and dissatisfaction on the part of many policy-makers, professionals, practitioners, academics and students, as to what exactly they were doing to, and with, the expanding number of children and young people diagnosed, assessed and labelled with an expanding variety of 'conditions' that usually led to exclusion in a variety of forms from mainstream education and subsequent employment opportunities. Psychological, medical and traditional pedagogic perspectives dominated the field, and turf wars between disciplines, professions, and academics intensified in the 1980s and continue to the present day, sometimes conducted with astonishing vituperation. Mental testing via IQ tests dominated the assessment process, although some psychologists, mindful of the reprehensible history of mental testing (see Kamin 1974; Tomlinson 1981) were reluctant to base exclusion on testing alone. In England until the 1970s it was a medical doctor who finally signed the form signifying that a child had a 'disability of body or mind', and in school there was a focus on remedial pedagogies for those regarded as backward or having learning difficulties. There was some reluctance to accept that different views of special education and its practices had validity, and sociological perspectives, as Len and I found, were not always popular.

Nevertheless, the critical sociological and political perspectives Len urged took hold during the 1980s. In 1982 he and I gave a paper in Boston on 'The Politics of Integration in English Special Education' at what was then the annual conference of the American Association of Mental Deficiency. We had an audience of around 20 inquisitiveness practitioners, enticed in by the coffee and doughnuts. This paper was later published in Barton and Tomlinson (1984). In the article we described the contradictory political decisions that removed children from mainstream education while ostensibly supporting the integration of as many children as possible, providing that it was economically efficient and those with special needs did not disrupt the education of others (DES 1980). At that time it was becoming clearer that any egalitarian policies inclining towards the merging of previously rejected groups into schools and the wider society were increasingly constrained by competition over priorities and resources. We continued to argue that given the inequalities inherent in the society and the dominant assumptions and practices in the education system, if integration was to have any significance it must be realised within changed

mainstream educational policies and practices. By the later 1980s education-
ists worldwide were debating the political and pedagogical consequences of
integration, soon to expand into notions of inclusion. In 1989 at a session on
the 'theory–practice link', organised by Tom Skrtic at the annual conference
of the Council for Exceptional Children in San Francisco, the audience for a
session on sociological and political perspectives had grown to 700 (Skrtic
1995). As the endeavour to explain 'what is going on' demanded the use of
more critical perspectives than the functional and pathological assumptions
behind much special educational practice, it was inevitable that some professionals and practitioners felt antagonistic to what appeared to be theorising for
its own sake or tainted with left-wing ideologies. Despite our jokes that much
theorising was more Groucho than Karl Marx, Len never assumed that theory
and practice were separate and he sought to develop 'a critical policy analysis
rooted in experience and in the processes of people's everyday lives' (Allen
and Slee 2008, 45). Critical views had to recognise that conflicts over power,
authority and vested interest were as endemic in the area of special education
as any other in the social world, and notions that professionals, administrators
and politicians were all working for the good of an ever-expanding clientele
of young people needed examination. It was in his 1988 book that Len argued
the tasks for a politics of special educational needs.

> First there needs to be a relentless systematic effort on the part of all interested
> parties in attempts to influence governments in relation to enhancing the lives
> and opportunities of people who are labelled in this way, particularly as the vast
> majority of these children and young people are … from lower socio-economic
> backgrounds. Second there is an essential revolutionary role to be undertaken in
> high-lighting the ways in which various policies and practices, including the
> assumptions and expectations underpinning daily interactions, contribute to the
> creation of handicaps and the resultant suffering which follows. Thirdly, in
> endeavouring to connect the personal with the political it is crucial that the
> thoughts of those with disabilities are made public and these become the basis
> for political alliances and endeavour. Lastly part of the work will be redefining
> the issues and moving the concern from a question of needs to that of rights.
> (Barton 1988, 7)

The theory and politics of disability

Len's clearest expression of the necessity for forging a link between political
action to bring about change and theoretical understanding of 'what is going
on' has been his support for disability rights and for bringing together disability rights advocates, academics – both abled and disabled – and practitioners.
Len and I did our teacher training at a time when the sight of a wheelchair in
public was as rare as the sight of a man pushing a baby buggy! Our reading
was exemplified by, for example, Jackson's benevolent account of the 'many
and varied (segregated) special schools and services that exist to provide suit-
able education for pupils who have any disability of body or mind' and the

careful description of the then 10 categories of handicapped children, and those considered unsuitable for education in school (Jackson 1969, 5). The sad case studies documented were all of working-class children and/or those living in poverty. The idea that those with any kind of a disability or 'learning difficulty' might actually have some influence over their lives or education was entirely lacking, as was any mention of social class and the selective nature of the education system A description of Len's engagement with the issues, organisations, legislation and controversies that over the ensuing years have begun to create more equitable lives, inclusion and voices for disabled people can be found in *Disability Studies Today* (Barnes, Oliver, and Barton 2002). Challenges to individual deficit, social deviance and medical models of disability came in the 1970s in the USA and Canada, but it was in Britain that the 'radical and controversial approach to theory and practice referred to as the social model of disability' was more fully developed (Barnes, Oliver, and Barton 2002, 4). While individual, medical, and personal tragedy views of disability had been supplemented from the 1970s by recognition that economic, social and cultural factors also 'produced' disability, it was disability activists who organised in the USA, the United Kingdom, Sweden and other countries and challenged orthodox views. A social interpretation of disability argued that whatever a person's perceived impairment, they were further disabled by society's failure to accommodate to their needs.

Len worked with many academic activists to provide venues and publication possibilities for inclusive education and living, and for disability activism and academic publication. While it may be invidious to select from these numerous friends and colleagues, perhaps mention should be made of Vic Finkelstein, who developed Britain's first disability studies course for the Open University in 1975 and was a founder of the Union of the Physically Impaired against Segregation, and long-time friend and disabled scholar Mike Oliver who firmly established a social model of disability (Oliver 1990). Other friends and activists included Colin Barnes, whose original study criticised the way disabled people were often regarded as no more important than vegetables (Barnes 1990), and Ayesha Vernon, blind scholar, formerly a senior lecturer at the University of Northumbria, who was the first to research the experiences of disabled minority women (Vernon 1998). Mention should also be made of Felicity Armstrong, co-writer and leader of the MA in Inclusive Education at the Institute of Education, and Roger Slee, friend and fellow professor who, when confronted by a bureaucrat who asserted that integration would mean a teacher having to toilet all 35 children in the class, replied that on the basis of probability, this could only happen in a school for the bladder disabled (Slee 1993, 1). A major aim of the journal *Disability and Society* was that it should develop a comprehensive theory of disability that took issue with medical and psychological theories. In 2007 Len encouraged debate in the review symposium in *Disability and Society* (vol. 22, no 2) in which an antagonistic argument between Oliver and Tom Shakespeare on the value of the social model of disability was played out, Oliver declaring that after this he would retire and devote himself to horses, poker and listening to Bob Dylan! (Allen and Slee 2008, 6). Mike and Len have over the years frequently been found at horse racing venues as well as academic or activist gatherings.

Challenging segregation and special needs

Len's early challenges to the notion that individual deficiencies of intellect, and disability as a personal misfortune created 'needs' for special education, either in segregated or a what initially passed for integrated settings, were not popular. Theories about the expansion of education systems in developed countries, which aimed to create a common public education system in which young people at all levels of development and ability would be included, originally ignored the exclusion of children from this common education on the grounds that they had special needs. The assumption, indeed, the common-sense view by those in control of education systems has always been that young people who are designated as low achievers, having learning difficulties and disabilities, or whose conduct is troublesome in classrooms, 'need' to be excluded to maintain the current aims and organisation of mainstream education. Len has always been clear that the major impediment to the ending of any form of segregated education and creation of genuine inclusive education is the form and purpose of existing mainstream education. Questioning powerful individuals, vested interests and ideologies that reproduce old and new reasons for the segregation or exclusion of groups of students has never been an easy task. On a global level Len has attributed recent and current rationales behind increasing selection and segregation, to the development of education as a competitive market underpinned by ideologies of economic rationality.

> Within this period of conservative restoration the impact of market ideologies has profoundly influenced how we think and talk about education. We view education through the lens of a form of economic rationality in which cost effectiveness, efficiency and value for money has entailed the generation of a more competitive, selective and socially divisive series of policies and practices, and globally the major purpose of education is the preparation of an economically productive, globally competitive workforce. (Barton 2004, 64)

Such a view raises the question, as it did in early industrialising societies, as to what the place is of those who may experience extra challenges in a climate of economically productive expectations. The need for mainstream education to exclude those who are regarded as interfering with the education of other more potentially productive students has led to a resurrection of various claims for segregation. Arguments are increasingly heard along the lines of: special schooling provides the type of education disabled and special students need, and protects them from the often harsh, cruel world of mainstream schooling and their non-disabled peers; normal pupils need protection from the damaging effect on their education of disabled children; special schools have teachers with special qualities of patience and dedication, and are administratively efficient with resources and support services (Barton 2004, 68). One of the powerful voices raised in support of sorting out the special into separate institutions again was Baroness Warnock who, having chaired the influential committee that in 1978 recommended an end to categories of hand-icap and more integration of the children who were now described as having special educational needs, produced a pamphlet in 2005, which repudiated her former views. She referred to 'possibly the most disastrous legacy of the 1978 Report, the concept of inclusion (formerly known as integration)' (Warnock 2005, 22). Her arguments were similar to those described above, and Len was one of the few who took issue with her pamphlet (Barton 2005). In particular he pointed out that although Warnock purported to offer a new look at special education she appeared ignorant of the central role disabled people and their organisation had played in the struggle for inclusion, and to 30 years of publi-cation by disabled activists, scholars and organisations. She made unsubstan-tiated claims that 'the desire to include children in similar institutions is a desire to treat them all the same' (Warnock 2005, 14) and recommended the setting up of 'special or specialist schools based on a new concept of inclu-sion' (2005, 14). Warnock has more recently turned her attention to support for selection and segregation at the other end of the supposed ability spectrum, suggesting grouping the 'high-flyers who love their subjects' into separate schools or classes, and regretting that:

> if a child goes to a school that does not think highly of education or academic precocity, and if the child has parents who are not interested either, the child will not flourish. (Warnock 2009, 7)

Len and I are in agreement that the fight against patronising educational elitism must be continuous.

Reflections on inclusive education

As Allen and Slee have noted;

> Len Barton's crucial part in the intellectual formation of inclusive education is widely acknowledged, and his definition, which spells out the requirement to increase participation and remove the exclusionary pressures (1997) is one which many of us regard as standard. (2008, 31)

But Len was acutely aware that hopes of including all those regarded up to the 1980s as handicapped or disabled were set back by the introduction of the super-category of special educational needs and 'integration' only for those children who could fit into existing school structures. The hegemonic view that in a world of global economic competitiveness national economies needed to pressure all young people to attain some pre-conceived 'standards', worked against beliefs in inclusive education and encouraged those who had always argued for selective and segregated schooling. Although from the 1990s the notion of inclusive education was globally promoted by international organisations[2]:

> The language of inclusion is being colonised by different groups and policies for all kinds of different purposes – many of them invested with values which far from embracing principles of equity and participation, are concerned with narrow notions of achievement and success as measured by attainment targets and underpinned by notions of competition and selection. (Barton and Armstrong 2007, 3)

In England, as in a number of other countries, a focus on the segregation of supposed higher-ability students, especially those described as gifted and talented, down-grades those considered merely average or less able. Internationally scholars seriously argue for differential models of giftedness and talent, which separates the extraordinarily gifted from the 'merely gifted' in ways reminiscent of nineteenth-century debates over gradations of mental retardation (Tomlinson 2008). Despite the manifold meanings attributed to the concept, inclusive education for Len was and remains a 'flagship ideal' that has encouraged many teachers, schools, local authorities, parents and communities to attempt changes in practices and cultures to those that are concerned with equity, human rights, social justice and the removal of discriminatory barriers. As an international movement hotly debated by educationalists and academics of all kinds, seized upon by governments to decide who should be excluded from certain kinds of education, and often encouraging empty promises and platitudes, Len and his co-writers have done a great service bringing together contributors worldwide to examine the meanings and practices of inclusive education in their respective countries.

> There is no one history of inclusive education, there is a diverse international movement, rooted in different social and historical conditions, but there is an international purpose behind those struggling and supporting inclusion. (Barton and Armstrong 2007, 4)

Inclusive education is part of the effort to counter the often pointless global struggles for economic dominance, and the encouragement of seemingly endless competition between institutions, teachers, parents and young people. Whatever the cultural, political, social or economic differences between countries, every society that aspires to create a decent, humane and effective system of education should think in terms of inclusion. Inclusion is an issue of equity and ethics, human rights and social justice, and also economic improvement.

Ways of knowing

In their book *Doing Inclusive Educational Research*, Allen and Slee interviewed a number of researchers in the area, including Len. They recorded that:

Initially, Len was our most coy respondent, articulating a hope that he had made an impact on somebody somewhere along the line (and we counted ourselves as at least two of these lucky individuals), but relaying his anxiety about academics' capacity for forgetting what it is like to be a learner. (Allen and Slee 2008, 85)

It can be said with some certainty that Len's work and teaching has had a profound effect on colleagues, teachers, students and, as noted, members of the disability movement. In his journal work he encouraged a wide range of perspectives and debates, and a respect for a diversity of intellectual ideas and practices. In dealing with the question of whether his work had made a difference, he pointed out again a major philosophical truth – that 'learning is a very disturbing process'. His goal was to challenge and unsettle conventional ways of knowing, and to provide others with the capacity to be both critical of accepted views and practices, and also self-critical. He is scornful of those who claim expertise in areas pertaining to disability or special education who arrogantly assume they can deny children access to mainstream education, and of a world where governments, and many academics and practitioners prefer to stick with traditional ideologies and practices, however offensive to recipients, rather than consider new perspectives and ways of knowing. A major satisfaction has been engagement with students. and he has recorded that 'I love teaching …and I've never had anything but an increasing desire to be a good teacher in a relationship where one earns respect from students and I have the benefit of learning from them' (Allen and Slee 2008, 85). Like many involved with 'special' and inclusive education over the years, Len regards academic publications with some scepticism and would argue for more direct political engagement. Perhaps, 'What on earth are all these publications doing in terms of any real change?' (Allen and Slee 2008, 86) is a question we should all be asking ourselves.

Notes

1. Harry Secombe was a well-known British comedian who also wore a fedora hat.
2. The United Nations General Assembly called in 1975 for full and equal participation of those regarded as disabled in a Declaration on the Rights of Disabled People, and by 2006 many countries had signed the International Convention on the Rights of Persons with Disabilities. The World Bank and UNESCO are committed to 'inclusive education for all' (UNESCO 1994)

References

Allen, J., and R. Slee. 2008. *Doing inclusive educational research*. Rotterdam: Sense Publishers.

Barnes, C. 1990. *The cabbage syndrome: The social construction of dependence.* Lewes: Falmer Press.

Barnes, C., M. Oliver, and L. Barton, eds. 2002. *Disability studies today*. Cambridge: Polity Press.

Barton, L., ed. 1988. *The politics of special educational needs.* Lewes: Falmer Press.

Barton, L. 1997. Inclusive education: Romantic, subversive or realistic. *International Journal of Inclusive Education* 1, no. 3: 231–42.

Barton, L. 2004. The politics of special education: A necessary or irrelevant approach. In *Education and the politics of (in) exclusion,* ed. L. Ware. New York: Peter Lang.

Barton, L. 2005. Special educational needs: An alternative look. Archive section: University of Leeds Disability Studies website. Sociology and Social Policy Department. www.leeds.ac.uk.

Barton, L., and F. Armstrong, eds. 2007. *Policy, experience and change: Cross-cultural reflections on inclusive education.* Dordrecht: Springer Books.

Barton, L., and S. Tomlinson, eds. 1981. *Special education: Policy, practices and social issues.* London: Harper and Row.

Barton, L., and S. Tomlinson, eds. 1984. *Special education and social interests.* London: Croom Helm.

DES. 1978. *Report of the Committee of Enquiry into the Education of Handicapped Children (The Warnock Report).* London: HMSO.

DES. 1980. *Special needs in education.* Cmnd 7996. London: HMSO.

Jackson, S. 1969. *Special education in England and Wales.* Oxford: Oxford University Press.

Kamin, L.J. 1974. *The science and politics of IQ.* Harmondsworth: Penguin Books.

Oliver, M. 1990. *The politics of disablement.* London: Macmillan. 2nd ed., 2010.

Skrtic, T., ed. 1995. *Disability and democracy: Reconstructing (special) education in post modernity.* New York: Teachers College Press.

Slee, R., ed. 1993. *Is there a desk with my name on it?* London: Falmer Press.

Tomlinson, S. 1981. *Educational subnormality; A study in decision-making.* London: Routledge and Kegan Paul.

Tomlinson, S. 2008. Gifted, talented and high ability: education for selection in a one-dimensional world. *Oxford Review of Education* 34, no. 1: 59–74.

UNESCO. 1994. *The Salamanca Statement and framework for action.* Paris: France.

Vernon, A. 1998. Understanding simultaneous oppression; The experience of disabled Black women in education and employment. PhD thesis, University of Leeds, UK.

Warnock, M. 2005. *Special educational needs: A new look.* London: Philosophy Society of Great Britain.

Warnock, M. 2009. Children need to be taught to think highly of education. *The Independent,* 29 July, p. 7.

Disability studies, disabled people and the struggle for inclusion

Mike Oliver[a] and Colin Barnes[b]

[a]University of Greenwich, London, UK; [b]Centre for Disability Studies, School of Sociology and Social Policy, University of Leeds, Leeds, UK and Department of Health and Social Sciences, University of Halmstad, Halmstad, Sweden

This paper traces the relationship between the emergence of disability studies and the struggle for meaningful inclusion for disabled people with particular reference to the work of a pivotal figure in these developments: Len Barton. It is argued that the links between disability activism and the academy were responsible for the emergence of disability studies and that this has had an important influence on mainstream sociology and social and educational policy nationally and internationally. It is evident, however, that the impact of these developments has been only marginal and that in light of recent concerns about the global economy, environmental change and unprecedented population growth, the need for meaningful inclusion is more urgent than ever and cannot be dependent on the work of a few key individuals for its success.

Introduction

The development of disability studies as an academic discipline is inextricably linked with the rise of the disabled people's movement that effectively began in the 1970s. In this paper we do not intend to describe this in any detail as it has been discussed elsewhere (Barnes, Oliver, and Barton 2002; Oliver 2009; Barnes and Mercer 2010). Instead we want to discuss the wider implications of this phenomenon for sociology, education and its impact on the lives of disabled people. In so doing we shall use mainly the words of Len Barton, who has played a pivotal role in these developments. Inevitably and unfortunately space will not permit us to discuss the contributions of others who have also been important (see, for example, Albrecht 1976; Finkelstein 1980, 1998: Tomlinson 1982, 1995; Oliver 1981, 1983, 1990; Barnes 1990, 1991, 2003; Davis 1995, 1997, 2006; Shakespeare 1998; Albrecht, Seelman, and Bury 2001). The paper is divided into three parts. We begin with a discussion of the relationship between disability studies, sociology and education policy.

Attention then centres on the links between the academy and activism. The final section examines the impact of these developments with reference to disability policy and practice.

Barton, in a recent interview to discuss the international journal *Disability and Society*, of which he was founding editor, provides a succinct description of the terrain we shall cover herein:

> The journal was created at a period when both nationally and internationally disabled people and their organisations were involved in serious struggles over the establishment of empowering conceptions of disability, rights, citizenship and independent living. Through the development of what is called the social model of disability, which is a creation of disabled people, the question of disability began to be understood as a form of social oppression, and it was connected to issues of equity, social justice and human rights, and as well, at this period, disability studies was beginning to emerge as a distinct study in higher education. (Barton 2009)

Unlike previous traditional individual, medical approaches, the social model breaks the causal link between impairment and disability. The 'reality' of impairment is not denied but is not the cause of disabled people's economic and social disadvantage. Instead, the emphasis shifts to how far, and in what ways, society restricts their opportunities to participate in mainstream economic and social activities rendering them more or less dependent. This approach has been a key influence on social policy in general, and disability policy in particular, although its influence on education policy has been considerably less.

Barton, however, has always attempted to open channels of communication in both academic and policy areas. He was not only founding editor of the journal referred to above but had the same pivotal role in the genesis and development of the *British Journal of the Sociology of Education*. Since the establishment of both journals, Barton has always tried to ensure that there was a dialogue between their respective areas of interest, although to begin with there was little enthusiasm for such a task:

> Mainstream sociology has historically shown little interest in the issue of disability … Sociologists have tended to accept the dominant hegemony with regard to viewing disability in medical and psychological terms. (Barton 1996, 6)

Hence, there was little interest in substantive areas such as education in general and special education in particular. Barton was unapologetic in both drawing attention to this situation as well as spelling out its implications for those who would listen:

> Within Britain, sociological analysis of, for example, special education is a relatively new development. An important basis for such work is that an understanding of the plight of vulnerable people gives some crucial insights into the nature of society. (Barton 1993, 235–236)

He was not solely drawing attention to the nature of society, however; he was also drawing attention to some of the central concerns of the sociological agenda since its foundation in the nineteenth century. Until the 1970s sociologists had been content to leave the personal tragedy halo that surrounded both special education and disability to others, but Barton insisted that sociological concerns about power and politics were essential to their creation and our understanding of them:

> ... there is an orthodoxy abroad which views any reference to the question of politics as being biased, irrelevant and counter-productive. This is particularly applicable to those who would seek to raise the question of politics in relation to special education policy or practice. To do so is to raise doubts about the nature of your commitment and whether you have the proper interests of individuals with learning difficulties in view. (Barton 1988, 5–6)

This orthodoxy was beginning to be challenged outside of the academy, however; some parents' groups were beginning to challenge special education policies and practices that usually segregated their children from the mainstream, often on the basis of irrelevant medical labels. Also disabled people were confronting and questioning professionally-led policies and practices that attempted to provide them with 'care and protection' but very little else. The debates that emerged in academia as a result of this took off in what has come to be called the inclusion/exclusion debate not just in education but in society as well.

The exclusion/inclusion debate

This debate began in education and was initially concerned about the location of children considered to have 'special educational needs' (SEN). Hence it was originally called the integration/segregation debate and focused almost exclusively on where these children should be educated; namely in special or regular mainstream schools. Barton, among others, began to insist however that this was far too narrow and that a broader range of educational, political, social and economic issues needed to be considered. So much so that new terminology was needed in order to move beyond the previous sterile discussions. Consequently the new term 'inclusion' appeared along with Barton's insistence that:

> Inclusive education is about the education of all children which necessitates serious changes, both in terms of society and its economic, social conditions and relations and in the schools of which they are a part. (Barton 1998b, 60)

The disabled people's movement had developed an analytical tool to assist in their political campaigns for a better life. We have already referred to this as the social model of disability, and it was based upon the simple idea that people were not disabled by the functional limitations of their impairments but by the external barriers that prevented their full participation in the societies in which they lived. Without ever calling it that, Barton's writings on education have always insisted that a social model approach should be an essential tool in changing the education system to a more inclusive one:

> Identifying institutional barriers to participation in education – in terms, for example, of the organisation and nature of the system of provision, the curriculum, pedagogy and assessment practice – this is an urgent and crucial task demanding serious and systematic attention. It is an essential part of the process of engagement that the struggle for inclusive policy and practice involves. (Barton 1998b, 61)

Despite these assertions, it is probably true to say that the social model has rarely been *explicitly* used as a tool for producing educational change.

The academy and activism

While the university has usually been a conservative political force at various times, it has on occasion played a key role in producing profound social and political change. Certainly in the latter half of the twentieth century we have seen radical ideas about integration and inclusion being developed both from within and outside academia, but we have also seen reactionary forces seeking to prevent changes from occurring. The rise of social movements promoting inclusion have forced these issues onto academic agendas and forced institutions at least to acknowledge the existence of these external agencies. This has occurred in the areas of race, gender, sexual orientation and disability and has spilled over into debates about education.

Within the academy, theorising and research activity have usually been seen as something for academics to engage in. Tentative attempts to promote alternative approaches based upon people's lived experiences have more often than not been dismissed as lacking objectivity. However, Barton has always insisted that academic debate and research stemming from it must take seriously the views of disabled people themselves:

> It is essential when considering the question of 'voice' in relation to educational research that we are aware of, and seek to learn, from the struggles disabled people have been and still are involved in outside the educational context. (Barton 1998a, 29)

The emergence of disability studies within the academy in recent years began to have an influence on traditional academic agendas:

> The increased interest in disability in the academy should not be surprising, given that there is now growing recognition that it raises a number of important theoretical and empirical questions at both the individual and structural level that are not easily answered with reference to established wisdom. Disability is both a common personal experience and a global phenomenon, with widespread

economic, cultural and political implications for society as a whole. (Barnes, Oliver, and Barton 2002, 2)

Since the 1970s we have seen the creation of more and more undergraduate and postgraduate courses in disability studies as well as the creation of several departments and professorial chairs in the subject. In the United Kingdom, for instance, there are now Chairs in disability-related studies at the Universities of Bristol, Glasgow, Dundee, de Montfort, Lancaster, Northumbria, Leeds, Manchester Metropolitan University and Brunel. Globally the rise in interest in disability studies has been is equally phenomenal. In 2010, for example, there are international disability studies conferences in Philadelphia, USA, in Montreal, Canada, in University of Tokyo, Japan and the UK's Disability Studies Network's fifth bi-annual event will be held 7–9 September at University of Lancaster. This conference is held every other year in conjunction with the Scandinavian Society for Disability Research conference, which is held in alternate years (Disability Studies Network 2010).

Until now, however, despite the influence of disability activism on the subject, one disabled activist has concluded that:

> It would seem that thus far the academic and research agenda and how far it is useful to activists has been to a large degree left to chance and the personal integrity of the individuals concerned. (Germon 1998 quoted in Barnes, Oliver, and Barton 2002, 258)

Yet as the discipline of disability studies becomes institutionalised within the academy, it raises a number of important concerns. Most notably is the issue of colonisation; will academics simply use the subject and the experience of disabled people for their own ends and to build their own careers or will a genuine partnership between the academy and activism emerge?

As mentioned earlier there has been a substantial growth in disability studies programmes across the world and a growing recognition within British sociology that disability is not simply a purely medical problem (Scambler 2004; Giddens 2006: Thomas 2007; Giddens and Sutton 2010). But, with few notable exceptions, the general trend has been toward a more pluralist approach commensurate with orthodox academic concerns rather than the development of a more comprehensive and radical socio/political analysis based around social model insights (Oliver and Barnes 2006; Oliver 2009). This is exemplified by the claim that the social model of disability is an 'outdated ideology' and that Britain's disabled people's movement is no longer representative of the disabled population as a whole (Shakespeare and Watson 2002; Shakespeare 2006).

Policy, practice and disabled people

The social model

Despite such assertions there is no doubt that our understandings of impairment and disability at the policy level have improved considerably as a result of the work described above and the contributions of key individuals like Len Barton for whom the social model has always been central to their work. Key to these understandings is the fact that while impairment may impose personal restrictions, disability is created by hostile cultural, social and environmental barriers. The disabled child in education may well have an impairment but his or her participation in school is restricted by an inaccessible curriculum, negative staff attitudes and physical barriers to getting around. This is clearly evident with reference to the fact that the social model of disability, as it is now called, is now widely recognised at both the national and international levels as the key to understanding and explaining the economic, political and social barriers encountered by disabled people.

Since the launch of the campaign for legislation to outlaw discrimination against disabled people in 1991 by the British Council of Disabled People – the UK's national umbrella for organisations controlled and run by disabled people themselves, and renamed the United Kingdom's Disabled People's Council in 2006 – the language of the social model, independent living and disability rights have become increasingly prominent in the publications produced by national and local government organisations and disability charities both large and small (Oliver and Barnes 2006). For example, the recent Cabinet Office report 'Improving the Life Chances of Disabled People' states clearly that:

'Disability' should be distinguished from 'impairment and ill health'

and defined as:

- disadvantage experienced by an individual …
- … resulting from barriers to independent living or educational, employment or other opportunities …
- … that impact on people with impairments and or ill health. (Prime Minister's Strategy Unit 2005, 8)

The Report also endorsed the importance of the development of policies to enable disabled people achieve independent living so that:

by 2025 disabled people have full opportunities and choices to improve their quality of life and be included and be respected as equal members of society. (Prime Minister's Strategy Unit 2005, 6)

At the European level, a study entitled 'Disability Policies in European Countries' by Vim van Oorschot and Bjorn Hvinden concluded that:

The thinking about disability associated with the Social Model (of disability) appears to have become more widely accepted. (Oorschot and Hvinden 2001, 9)

This is clearly reflected in recent European Union (EU) policy statements on disability, as indicated below:

The EU also sees disability as a social construct. The EU social model of disability stresses the environmental barriers in society which prevent the full participation of people with disabilities in society. These barriers must be removed. (European Commission of the European Communities 2003, 4)

Further afield. Disabled People's International, the international equivalent of the United Kingdom's Disabled People's Council, adopted a similar approach at its inception in 1981 (Driedger 1989). Its influence at the international level, particularly within the United Nations (UN), is indisputable. A social model perspective is implicit if not explicit in various UN documents. The UN 'Standard Rules on the Equalisation of Opportunities for People with Disabilities' (UN Enable 2005) and 'The Convention on the Rights of Persons with Disabilities' (UN 2006) are but two examples (Hurst and Albert 2006). Also, a social model perspective played a key role in the recent 'Rethinking Care from Disabled People's Perspectives' initiative sponsored by the World Health Organisation's Disability and Rehabilitation Team; a two-year project and conference that involved professionals, disabled people, and their families from all over the world (World Health Organisation 2001).

Policy and practice

All of this has led to a number of policy initiatives that at face value appear to address many of the concerns of disabled people and their organisations. In the United Kingdom, for instance, in response to the campaign mentioned above, the Disability Discrimination Act came onto the statute books in 1995 to outlaw discrimination against disabled people. This was followed a year later by the Community Care (Direct Payments) Act to legalise cash payments from local authorities to enable disabled individuals to employ their own personal assistants rather than rely on staff appointed and controlled by professionally led agencies such as local authorities and National Health Service trusts.

Following the election of the New Labour Government in 1997, the Disability Rights Task Force was established in 1999 followed in 2000 by the Disability Rights Commission with the support of the large disability charities and key figures in the disabled people's movement. In 2001 anti-discrimination legislation was extended to include education: The Special Educational Needs and Disability Act (SENDA). The Disability Rights Commission along with the Equal Opportunities Commission and the Commission for Racial Equality was abolished in 2006 and replaced by the Equality and Human Rights Commission with a remit to cover all forms of discrimination including religion and age. Unfortunately, as we indicate below, the Commission has not made a promising start.

After publication of the *Improving Life Chances* report in 2005, the government introduced the 'Disability Equality Duty'. In contrast to previous policies, this was conceived as a proactive measure that requires all public institutions to produce a 'Disability Equality Scheme' outlining plans to make the necessary changes in all policy and practices to facilitate disabled people's inclusion. The intention was that these schemes are reviewed and amended every three years until equality is achieved. The responsibility for ensuring that public organisations and institutions fulfil their obligations under the Disability Equality Duty was the responsibility of the Equality and Human Rights Commission. However, the impact of these initiatives has been only marginal. This is due in large part to the fact that all the legislative measures mentioned above lack teeth and therefore have not been properly enforced. Monitoring and enforcement have been almost none existent.

Research commissioned by the government's Office of Disability Issues on the practices of 35 public authorities across seven policy sectors, including housing, education, health, environment, transport, culture and criminal justice, found that at best the mainstreaming of disability issues had been 'only partly achieved in some organisations, while others have a long way to go' (Ferrie et al. 2008, 14). Similar stories are evident across Europe and the rest of the world (see, for example, Stone 1999; Priestley 2001; Barnes and Mercer 2005; Albert 2006; Katsui 2006; Inclusion Europe 2008; Clements and Read 2008; Yeo and Bolton 2008).

Education

In the United Kingdom, the idea of educating disabled children in mainstream school environments had been around since the Education Act (1944). None-theless it created 11 medically based classifications of children and, despite its lukewarm endorsement of integration, facilitated the expanded segregative practices of the past the 'special school' system, which had its roots in the eighteenth century. Hence special schools flourished in the post-1939–1945 war period and continued to expand until the early 1990s despite the publica-tion of the Warnock Report (Warnock 1978) and its implementation through the Education Act (1981).

Following the longstanding critique of segregated educational systems for children and students labelled with 'SEN' (see, for example, Tomlinson 1982, 1995; Barton and Tomlinson 1984; Barton 1988; Rieser and Mason 1990; Oliver 1990, 2000; Barton and Armstrong 2001, 2007), the principle of inclusive education was endorsed in official documents both nationally and internationally (see, for example, UNESCO 1994, 2006, 2007; Department for Education and Employment 1998; UN 2006).

In 1997 the Department for Education and Employment endorsed the UNESCO *Salamanca Statement and Framework for Action on Special Needs*:

> This statement calls on the international community to endorse the approach of inclusive schools by implementing practical and strategic changes. (UNESCO 1994, 1)

This is based on the assertion that

> regular schools with this inclusive orientation are the most effective means of combating discriminatory attitudes, creating welcoming communities, building an inclusive society and achieving education for all. (UNESCO 1994, 1)

Yet despite apparent initial enthusiasm for such an approach by the Labour Government of 1997 and the introduction of SENDA in 2000, progress has been slow. For instance, the proportion of all children attending special schools, that rose to just under 1% at the start of the 1980s, has subsequently declined to only 0.8% (Rustemier and Vaughan 2005; Department for Education and Skills [DfES] 2007). The number of special schools fell from 1830 in 1990/91 to 1391 in 2006/07 (DfES 2007). Moreover, these figures mask considerable variation with segregation increasing slightly in one-third of local education authorities in England (Rustemier and Vaughan 2005).

But mainstream schools are not inclusive, and segregation into special units or classes is not uncommon. With few notable exceptions the dominant discourse emphasises academic success and 'ableist' values (Tomlinson 1995; Benjamin 2003). These are often reinforced by poor environmental access, particularly in secondary schools and colleges (Audit Commission 2002), and restricted opportunities for participation in out-of-school activities (Gray 2002). Major concerns revolve around the continued dominance of standards agendas and examination assessment criteria that prioritise outcomes over process and disregard the appropriateness of an inclusive curriculum (Ofsted 2004; Qualifications and Curriculum Authority 2004).

A longstanding criticism of special educational provision is that it does not provide disabled children with the qualifications and skills for adulthood. Recent research indicates that over 25% of disabled adults have no qualifications or marketable skills whatsoever; more than twice that for non-disabled peers (Office of National Statistics 2005). This gap is particularly evident for those labelled with 'learning difficulties' or 'mental health problems'. While special school results have improved over the past decade, the average examination points score of 50 compares very unfavourably with the 361 average for regular schools (DfES 2007). Children rated as 'SEN' in mainstream schools are more than twice as likely as special school pupils to take GCSE or GNVQ examinations (Audit Commission 2002).

Moreover, despite several international initiatives to ensure that children with accredited impairments are not excluded from mainstream schools following the *Salamanca Statement,* there remains a divergence of views on the meaning of inclusion. Consequently, despite some notable successes (Rieser 2008), many disabled children are educated in segregated school environments (Miles and Singal 2008). Also, there is substantial evidence that disabled children's exclusion from all forms of education is commonplace. Indeed, in some countries disabled girls are denied all of formal schooling. In others, children with 'intellectual disabilities' are considered uneducable

(UNESCO 1995). A recent EFA monitoring report suggests that globally only 10% of disabled children are in school (UNESCO 2007). In the United Kingdom, all disabled children are officially considered educable; consequently there are no known figures for those who may be excluded.

As Barton and others have repeatedly argued, an inclusive education system is a necessary prerequisite for an inclusive society.

Concluding comments

In this paper we have argued that the early development of disability studies was due primarily to the activities of academics such as Len Barton and their links with disability activism and the disabled people's movement – and that these developments have had an important influence on mainstream sociology, social policy and educational policies at both the national and international levels. But whilst the foundations for meaningful change have clearly been made, progress has been limited and the reality of an inclusive society seems as far away as ever. This is especially worrying as both the United Kingdom and the rest of the world face a series of unprecedented challenges that threaten to undermine any hope of future economic, political and social stability and progress toward a truly inclusive global society. Examples include the widening gulf between rich and poor within and across nation-states, overpopulation and environmental degradation (Oliver and Barnes 1998, 2006). If the contributions of committed individuals like Len Barton are not to be wasted, then as we move ever further into the twenty-first century the academy and the disabled people's movement will need to form a much more comprehensive and committed partnership than they have managed so far. This is simply because as Barton pointed out over a decade ago:

> ... there is now an urgency about the need for further attention being given to the development of a political analysis which is inspired by a desire for transformative change and that constitutes hope at the centre of struggles for inclusivity. (Barton 1998b, 53)

Whether the academic community, the disabled people's movement and its allies have the commitment or capacity to rise to this challenge has yet to be seen.

References

Albert, B., ed. 2006. *In or out of the mainstream? Lessons from research on disability and development cooperation.* Leeds: The Disability Press.

Albrecht, G.L. 1976. *The sociology of physical disability and rehabiolitation.* Pittsburgh, PA: The University of Pittsburgh Press.

Albrecht, G.L., K.D. Seelman, and M. Bury, eds. 2001. *Handbook of disability studies.* London: Sage.

Audit Commission. 2002. *Special educational needs – A mainstream issue.* London: Audit Commission.

Barnes, C. 1990. *Cabbage syndrome: The social construction of dependence.* Lewes: Falmer Press. http://www.disability-archive.leeds.ac.uk/.

Barnes, C. 1991. *Disabled people in Britain and discrimination.* London: Hurst and Co. in association with the British Council of Organisations of Disabled People. http://www.disability-archive.leeds.ac.uk/.

Barnes, C. 2003. Disability studies: what's the point? Keynote address presented at the Disability Studies Conference, 3 September, in University of Lancaster, UK. http://www.disability-archive.leeds.ac.uk/.

Barnes, C., and G. Mercer, eds. 2005. *The social model of disability – Europe and the majority world.* Leeds: The Disability Press.

Barnes, C., and G. Mercer. 2010: *Exploring disability: A sociological introduction.* 2nd ed. Cambridge: Polity.

Barnes, C., M. Oliver, and L. Barton, eds. 2002. *Disability studies today.* Cambridge: Polity.

Barton, L., ed. 1988. *The politics of special educational needs.* Lewes: Falmer.

Barton, L. 1993. The struggle for citizenship; The case for disabled people. *Disability and Society* 6, no. 3: 235–48.

Barton, L. 1996. Sociology and disability: Some emerging issues. In *Disability and society: Emerging issues and insights,* ed. L. Barton, 3–17. London: Longman.

Barton, L. 1998a. Developing an emancipatory research agenda: Possibilities and dilemmas. In *Articulating with difficulty: Research voices in inclusive education,* ed. P. Clough and L. Barton, 29–40. London: Paul Chapman Publishing.

Barton, L. 1998b. Sociology, disability studies and education. In *The disability reader: Social science perspectives,* ed. T. Shakespeare, 53–65. London: Cassell.

Barton, L. 2009. Transcript of audio interview with Professor Len Barton. www.informaworld.com/smpp/educationarena_interviewonline_interview5~db= educ.

Barton, L., and F. Armstrong. 2001. Disability, education and inclusion: Cross cultural issues and dilemmas. In *Handbook of disability studies,* ed. G.L. Albrecht et al., 693–710. Thousand Oaks, CA: Sage.

Barton, L., and F. Armstrong, eds. 2007. *Policy experience and change: Cross cultural reflections on inclusive education.* Dordrecht, The Netherlands: Springer.

Barton, L., and S. Tomlinson, eds. 1984. *Special education and political issues.* London: Croom Helm.

Benjamin, S. 2003. What counts as success? Hierarchical discourses in a girls' comprehensive school. *Discourse* 24, no. 1: 105–18.

Clements, L., and J. Read, eds. 2008. *Disabled people and the right to life: The protection and violation of disabled people's most basic human rights.* London: Routledge.

Davis, L.J. 1995. *Enforcing normalcy: Disability, deafness, and the body.* London: Verso.

Davis, L.J., ed. 1997. *The disability studies reader.* London: Routledge.

Davis, L.J., ed. 2006. *The disability studies reader.* 2nd ed. London: Routledge.

Department for Education and Employment. 1998. *Excellence for all children: Meeting special educational needs.* London: DfEE. http://www.dfes.gov.uk/consultations/downloadableDocs/45_1.pdf.

Department for Education and Skills. 2007. *Education and training statistics for the UK, 2007.* London: DfES.

Department of Health. 2009. *Shaping the future of care together.* London: DoH. http://www.dh.gov.uk/en/Consultations/Liveconsultations/DH_102339 accessed 5th January 2010.

Disability Studies Network. 2010. Disability Studies Conference: 5th Biannual Disability Studies Conference, Lancaster University, UK. http://www.disability-studies.net/?content=3 (accessed February 26, 2010).

Driedger, D. 1989. *The last civil rights movement.* London: Hurst and Co.

European Commission of the European Communities. 2003. *Equal opportunities for people with disabilities: A European action plan.* Communication from the Commission to the Council, The European Parliament, The European Economic and Social Committee and the Committee of the Regions, October 30. Brussels: European Commission. http://eur-lex.europa.eu/LexUriServ/LexUriServ.do?uri=COM:2003:0650:FIN:EN:PDF.

Ferrie, J., J. Lerpiniere, K. Paterson, C. Pearson, K. Stalker, and N. Watson. 2008. *An in depth analysis of the implementation of the Disability Equality Duty in England.* London: Office of Disability Issues.

Finkelstein, V. 1980. *Attitudes and disabled people: Issues for discussion.* New York: World Rehabilitation Fund. http://www.disability-archive.leeds.ac.uk/.

Finkelstein, V. 1998: Emancipating disability studies. In *Disability studies: Social science perspectives,* ed. T. Shakespeare, 28–49. London: Cassell. http://www.disability-archive.leeds.ac.uk/.

Germon P. 1998. Activists and academics: Part of the same or a world apart. In *The disability reader: Social science perspectives,* ed. T. Shakespeare, 245–55. London: Cassell.

Giddens, A. 2006. *Sociology.* 6th ed. Cambridge: Polity.

Giddens, A., and P. Sutton, eds. 2010. *Sociology: Introductory readings.* 3rd ed. Cambridge: Polity.

Gray, P. 2002. *Disability discrimination in education: A review of the literature on discrimination across the 0–19 age range.* London: Disability Rights Commission.

Hurst, R., and B. Albert. 2006. The social model of disability: Human rights and development cooperation. In *In or out of the mainstream? Lessons from research on disability and development cooperation,* ed. B. Albert, 24–39. Leeds: The Disability Press.

Inclusion Europe. 2008. *The specific risks of discrimination against persons in situations of major dependence or with complex needs: Report of a European study, Volume 3: Country reports.* Brussels: Inclusion Europe. http://www.inclusion-europe.org/documents/CNS%20Volume%201.pdf.

Katsui, H. 2006. Human rights and disabled people in the South. In *Vammaisten Ihmisoikeuksista Etäiiä,* ed. A. Teittinen, 86–119. Helsinki: Vliopistopaino. http://www.disability-archive.leeds.ac.uk/.

Miles, S., and N. Singal. 2008. The education for all and inclusive education debate. *International Journal of Inclusive Education.* http://www.leeds.ac.uk/disability-studies/archiveuk/miles/IJIE_MilesandSingal_resubmission.pdf.

Office of National Statistics. 2005. *National statistics: Special educational needs in England.* London: ONS. http://dfes.gov.uk/rsgateway/DB/SFR/s000584/SFR24-2005.pdf (accessed November 10, 2006).

Ofsted. 2004. *Special educational needs and disability: Towards inclusive schools.* London: Ofsted.

Oliver, M. 1981. A new model of the social work role in relation to disability. In *The handicapped person: A new perspective for social workers,* ed. J. Campling, 19–32. London: RADAR. http://www.leeds.ac.uk/disability-studies/archiveuk/index. html.

Oliver, M. 1983. *Social work with disabled people.* Basingstoke: Macmillan.

Oliver, M. 1990. *The politics of disablement.* Tavistock: Macmillan. http://www.disability-archive.leeds.ac.uk/.

Oliver, M. 2000. *Decoupling education from the economy in a capitalist society.* ://www.disability-archive.leeds.ac.uk/.

Oliver, M. 2009. *Understanding disability: From theory to practice.* 2nd ed. Tavistock: Palgrave.

Oliver, M., and C. Barnes. 1998. *Social policy and disabled people: From exclusion to inclusion.* London: Longman.

Oliver, M., and C. Barnes. 2006. Disability politics: Where did it all go wrong. In *Coalition,* 8–13. Manchester: Greater Manchester Coalition of Disabled People.

Oorschot, V., and B. Hvinden. 2001. Introduction: Toward convergence?: Disability policies in Europe. In *Disability policies in European societies,* ed. V. Oorschot and B. Hivnden, 3–12. The Hague: Kluwer Law International.

Peck, S. 2009. Rieser's reservations on ratification. In *Disability now,* 18. April 7. London: Scope.

Priestley, M., ed. 2001: *Disability and the life course: Global perspectives.* Cambridge: Cambridge University Press.

Prime Minister's Strategy Unit. 2005. *Improving the life chances of disabled people: Final report.* London: PMSU, Cabinet Office. http://www.cabinetoffice.gov.uk/strategy/work_areas/disability.aspx.

Qualifications and Curriculum Authority. 2004. *Inclusive learning: 2002/03 annual report on curriculum and assessment.* London: QCA.

Rieser, R. 2008. *Implementing inclusive education: A Commonwealth guide to implementing Article 24 of the UN Convention on the Rights of People with Disabilities.* London: Commonwealth Secretariat.

Rieser, R., and M. Mason. 1990. *Disability equality in the classroom: A human rights issue.* London: Inner London Education Authority.

Rustemier, S., and M. Vaughan. 2005. *Segregation trends – LEAs in England 2002–2004.* Bristol: Centre for Studies on Inclusive Education.

Scambler, G. 2004. Re-framing stigma: Felt and enacted stigma and challenges to the sociology of chronic and disabling conditions. *Social Theory and Health* 2, no. 1: 29–46.

Shakespeare, T., ed. 1998. *Disability studies: Social science perspectives.* London: Cassell.

Shakespeare, T. 2006. *Disability rights and wrongs.* London: Routledge.

Shakespeare, T., and N. Watson. 2002. The social model of disability: an outmoded ideology. *Research in Social Science and Disability* 2: 9–28. http://www.leeds.ac.uk/disability-studies/archiveuk/index.html.

Stone, E., ed. 1999. *Disability and development: Learning from action and research on disability in the majority world.* Leeds: The Disability Press.

Thomas, C. 2007. *Sociologies of disability and illness: Contested ideas in disability studies and medical sociology.* Basingstoke: Palgrave Macmillan.

Tomlinson, S. 1982. *A sociology of special education.* London: Routledge and Kegan Paul.

Tomlinson, S. 1995. *Machine and professional bureaucracies: Barriers to inclusive education.* http://www.disability-archive.leeds.ac.uk/.

UN Enable. 2005. Enable: Standard rules, overview. United Nations. www.un.org/esa/socdev/enable/dissre00.

UNESCO. 1994. *The Salamanca Statement and framework for action on special needs education.* Paris: UNESCO.

UNESCO. 1995. *Overcoming obstacles to the integration of disabled people.* London: Disability Awareness in Action.

UNESCO. 2006. *EFA global monitoring report 2007: Early childhood care and education.* Paris: UNESCO.

UNESCO. 2007. *EFA Global monitoring report 2008: Education for all by 2015. Will we make it?* Paris: UNESCO.

United Nations. 2006. Convention on the rights of persons with disabilities. http://www.un.org/disabilities/convention/conventionfull.shtml.

Warnock, M. 1978. *Report of the Committee of Enquiry into the education of handicapped children and young people.* London: HMSO.

World Health Organisation. 2001. *Rethinking care from disabled people's perspectives.* Geneva: WHO. http://www.disability-archive.leeds.ac.uk/authors_list.asp?AuthorID=188&author_name=World+Health+Organisation+Disability+and+Rehabilitation+Team.

Yeo, R., and A. Bolton. 2008. *'I don't have a problem, the problem is theirs'. The lives and aspirations of Bolivian disabled people in words and pictures.* Leeds: The Disability Press. http://www.disability-archive.leeds.ac.uk/.

Revisiting the politics of special educational needs and disability studies in education with Len Barton

Roger Slee

School of Curriculum, Pedagogy & Assessment, Institute of Education, University of London, London, UK

This brief essay celebrates the work of Len Barton. Drawing from a range of his texts, interviews and presentations, the essay attempts to demonstrate the importance of Barton's work in establishing foundations for the related fields of disability studies in education and inclusive education by revealing the politics of special educational needs and the requirement for a sociological analysis of traditional special education as a force for the disablement of vulnerable students. The essay will illustrate the centrality and the particularity of the complex relationships between research, teaching, learning and activism in the thinking and work of Professor Barton.

Introduction

Considering the work of Len Barton requires attention to more than text alone. For that reason I will draw upon Len and others' work, from an interview Julie Allan and I conducted in 2005 with him, and intersperse this with stories to characterize that work of Len's that is not textual. It is also difficult to write about a person who, while a public intellectual, is a very private person whose essence is reflected in and deflected by genuine humility. With this in mind I will write about the progress of critiques of special education and the way in which Len Barton has helped many of us to adopt and adapt sociological tools to develop a critical approach to thinking about inclusive education and disability studies in education.

I was fortunate to have been invited by Len to participate in an annual disability studies conference, first in Hull and later in Leeds. The conferences bore many of the hallmarks of Len's other major conference;[1] the International Sociology of Education Conference, which many still refer to as the

Westhill Conference although its location has shifted at least four times since the Birmingham days. It was a small group of people, maybe 12–20 of us. The draft papers were circulated ahead of the conference and were to be read before we met. People were asked not to read their paper, they were encouraged instead to make a brief introduction to the issues they wanted to raise and speak of the difficulties the paper had raised for them. Although the theme was set, the topics within that theme were expansive. Moreover the forum was not of one mind. For the neophyte academic this was an intimidating sociological feast. On offer was a range of sociological perspectives, structuralism to post-structuralism, with which to analyse the conditions and relations of disablement. Debate was intense, often fiery. The language deployed was an informal amalgam of the sociological imagination with the rich vernacular of the football terraces. Len Barton and Mike Oliver's presence ensured frequent allusions to those great social commentators Cohen and Zimmerman. After sometimes-fierce exchanges, people would come together at the meal table or at the bar to joke, argue and (sadly) to sing. Reflecting on Len's role as convener, patterns emerge. He would welcome people, thank them for the preparation and then give some brief remarks on the theme. Mostly these remarks were interrogative.

Let me also depict another hallmark of these meetings. Links between the discussions and the disability movement's political struggle were omnipresent. That was indeed the point – praxis – 'partisan research' (Troyna 1994). The sociological purpose was always described in relation to the disabled people's movement and to the struggle against disabling barriers. How could it be otherwise when Mike Oliver, Colin Barnes or Mairian Corker would cut through someone's surfeit of words to ask what difference this would make to the lives of disabled people? At one of the Hull conferences Len had invited Johnny Crescendo, a disabled singer, songwriter and activist, to join us. He would lead the singing at night and pull folk up short in the daytime discussions when meaning hid behind a thicket of academic jargon. At these meetings Len would sit and listen, his pencil and notebook at hand. Rarely would he speak unless to ask an unsettling question to dispel intellectual foreclosure. These conferences were writing workshops that always generated publication, lifetime friendships and enduring debates across the field of disability studies.

Years later Julie Allan and I were working on a project that gave us the opportunity to interview key researchers, writers and activists in the field of inclusive education (Allan and Slee 2008). Len was an obvious target for our interrogations. His responses to our questions revealed a great deal about his work as a teacher, scholar and activist. Indeed this forms an indivisible trilogy that guides his work, as the following lengthy extract from the interview underscores.

> … it is very important when I think about the academic world … that one recognizes the centrality of the relationship between teaching and research. If I

think of the journals, for example, every journal I have ever created has come out of my teaching. It's because I got more involved in the teaching process and thinking about the issues in these areas, I recognized a greater need for a forum, a forum that would represent the possibility of a wide range of perspectives engaging on similar issues. So it wasn't a question of a single orthodoxy, as some people suggested, that I had developed. Rather, if you read any of the journals you'll see there a whole range of different approaches from postmodernist to Marxist. ... It was about engaging in a process that would establish a system of relationships and collegiality that would be lasting and that would be valuable not only for me but for the field. ... It was important that in one's own practice one illustrated the importance of community and illustrated the importance of respect for diversity of intellectual, pragmatic ideas and so forth. ... in disability studies there is the added difference that I felt, and still do in many ways, quite vulnerable in terms of my own ignorance and my own misunderstandings of both disabled people and their experiences, their feelings, their desires and therefore it was quite a difficult experience. It has been a perennial issue for me and one that I feel quite unclear about at times as to the degree to which one's been able to be a non-disabled person, be a non-disabled academic person, and yet have a relationship and affiliation to disabled people of the disability movement. It is even more difficult for disabled scholars. They are caught between such terrible pressures of having to try to gain recognition and status within the academic community and movement and disability activism. (Barton 2005, 1–2)

There are a number of important overarching themes that recurred in his answers to our questions about his research in disability studies. These themes form the structure of this short essay. The themes are:

- Affirming the relationship between teaching, research and activism.
- The question of voice.
- Struggle, urgency and the challenge of writing.
- The necessity for humility as a social scientist/activist.

Affirming the relationship between teaching, research and activism

Re-reading that extract from our transcript of the interview with Len, I am struck by his emphasis on the relationship between research and teaching and learning; in particular, his notion of the teacher as learner. It is worth pursuing this further to show the particularity of his conception of the good teacher:

I've never had anything but an increasing desire to be a good teacher in a relationship where one earns respect from the students and I have the benefit of learning from them. But I want students to lead me. I am now absolutely clear, I became clear about this gradually, but I am clear about it now, with one perennial and profound understanding and that is they must never see themselves as anything but a learner and we're all learners together. We are at different stages of the learning continuum, but there's never a moment when I am not a learner. That process is a basis for the removing of arrogance ... (Barton 2005, 3)

The conferences, disability studies and sociology of education alike reflected an approach to teaching and learning. They provided a forum to encourage dialogical encounters (Friere 1972) in order to reframe questions to lead research and teaching across important social and educational issues. The conferences, says Barton, were about his:

> ... desire to get Olive Banks, get Geoff Whitty, get Andy Hargreaves[2] (key figures in the development of the sociology of education) in the same room addressing a similar theme ... to get some serious critical engagement ... I wanted a much more open dialogical relationship between the people from different positions. It was great. It was really important and from those things also came the journal (British Journal of Sociology of Education). (Barton 2005, 2)

Teaching and learning, like sociology itself, are fundamentally social acts (Vygotsky 1962; Barton 1996, 4). Noteworthy is Barton's multidimensional conception of relationships for learning. Let me simply précis them.

The first element of the relationships that entwine teaching and learning for Barton is the necessity to bring people together to struggle together, 'to argue about a sentence' (Barton 2005, 2) and transcend 'the individualism and the unhealthy competitiveness which I had experienced with a great deal of pain in my school life, so I found it difficult within the academic world as well' (Barton 2005, 2).

The second relational element is the importance of expanding the analytic toolkit by enlisting a range of perspectives in the research. This is achieved by establishing respectful forums for critique across different paradigms and across different identities (Barton 1996, 10). In this way the conferences, the journals, the tutorials, the edited books each provide a fearless platform for the struggle of ideas to refine our questions in the service of social change. This is, as Connell (1993, 124) observes, a 'deeply uncomfortable' research project. The Disability and Society Conference at Ashford in Kent in September 1996 summoned a new level of intellectual and emotional tension across the disabled people's movement in the United Kingdom as the social model bumped up against the feminist and postmodern voices of researchers such as Corbett, Corker, Shakespeare and Watson (Barton and Oliver 1997). These tensions have persisted to expand the field of disability studies internationally.

There is a third element to note. At the heart of Barton's work is the relationship between the research endeavour and the political project:

> I think there has been an increasing desire and commitment to try to understand and work on the purpose of research that is other than merely confirming academic interests and concerns. I think disability studies for example and some of the issues in sociology of education have been a wonderful confirmation of this in the sense that I do believe increasingly that my interest is not only in understanding the world but to see some change and change me in that process. One of the interests has been clearly to try to understand the nature of discrimination in its many complex and contradictory forms. (Barton 2005, 3)

Like other critical sociologists and educators, his work characterizes Marx's dictum that the point is not discussion, interpretation and a prosperous academic career; the point is to work in the service of overcoming discrimination and oppression. A clear exposition of this theme is taken up in his essay in *Articulating with Difficulty: Research Voices in Inclusive Education* (Clough and Barton 1998), where he enlists Oliver's challenge to the predominantly oppressive social relations of research (Oliver 1992, 102). Barton argues:

> He [Oliver] … is seeking to encourage … a fundamental shift in the ways in which we think about research, including the purpose, process and outcomes of these activities. He wants to see the introduction of a different set of social relations of research production which will provide the possibility for a more enabling, or what he terms 'emancipatory', form of research activity. (Barton 1998, 31–32)

Finding unity and authenticity in the research/activist alliance is not straightforward. Posturing is easy. Wrapping oneself up in a flag of Che Guevara and talking of comrades and emancipation does not a revolutionary make. In this respect, the gurus of critical pedagogy test the patience of the researcher activist as envisaged by Barton and Oliver. Attempting 'to get a firmer grip on interpretations of "empowerment" in educational research discourses', Troyna (1994, 5) has 'explore[d] some of the taken-for-granted assumptions associated with the term'. In doing so, he reveals the often '… illusory and obfuscatory, but nonetheless intuitively appealing, rhetoric of critical pedagogy where empowerment often takes centre stage' (Troyna 1994, 5). At the Sociology of Education Conference in Sheffield in 1993, Troyna issued a challenge for us to engage in an interrogation of the 'types and configurations of power relations which suffuse researchers' understanding of what "empowerment" might look like' (Troyna 1994, 20). Barry Troyna's lasting contributions to anti-racist education and to defending the character and rigour of 'partisan research' against repeated critiques from Foster, Gomm, and Hammersley (1996), and Hammersley (2000) found support from Barton's inclusive educational project.

'The emancipatory role', wrote Barton (1996, 5), 'is not only concerned with demonstrating different forms of discrimination and under what conditions they develop, but also doing something about it'. To explore this further I turn to my second meta-theme that infuses and makes distinctive his body of work. Here I speak of Barton's enduring insistence on questions of voice as central to building a research programme or project with potential to make a difference to the unequal social relations of research.

The question of voice

Professor Barton was on an interview panel for a position I had applied for as a relatively young researcher. He asked me if I could talk to the panel about my consideration of the question of voice in my research. I vaguely remember speaking for a long time (it is what is done in this trade when you do not have a real answer). Perhaps I remember speaking vaguely for a long time. In subsequent conversations with him, through attending his classes and teaching with him, I came to learn some of the possibilities that present themselves through the consideration of this question.

The key to understanding the concept of voice is in our ability to listen.

Julie: And if I could just pursue this notion of working with disabled people, what are the particular difficulties of working with disabled people in the research process?

Len: A major difficulty is learning what it means to listen. We have a perennial problem as academics and that is we've got a position on everything. We talk whereas listening to people is such a profoundly significant issue in relation to working in a research context with disabled people in particular. You can't rush that. It requires time and emotional and intellectual energy in order to actually seriously engage with that.

The language you use is particularly important because within the academic world you develop a series of discourses and a lexicon that becomes taken for granted and therefore for those people for quite understandable and significant reasons haven't a clue what you are talking about. (Barton 2005, 7)

Jenny Corbett (1998, 55), a colleague of Len's at the Institute of Education, contends that the '… issue of voice in emancipatory research is complex and multi-layered'. She unravels the complexity for us by suggesting three layers for examining the issue of voice in emancipatory research:

1. Which discipline (psychology or sociology) or specific model (e.g. the social model of disability) gains prominence in setting the tenor of the research framework and key issues;
2. Dilemmas in sample selection, in deciding how to listen and what to hear;
3. The need to provide a means of expression beyond the conventional which most accurately conveys the perceptions and experiences of vulnerable people whose apparent ideas are open to interpretive distortion and abuse. (Corbett 1998, 55)

A recent example of his insistence on the centrality of disabled people's voices and disability research in questions of educational exclusion and inclusion was his reluctant yet politically strident response to Dame Mary Warnock's (2005) 'new look' at special educational needs:

In trying to understand the claims of the author, we are left with the overwhelming feeling that this document is a mixture of important historical insights, but also a reflection of naivety, arrogance and ignorance on the part of the author? How have we come to this conclusion? … one would expect some careful discussion of the ideas of those who represent an alternative perspective. Instead, we have no discussion of a serious nature with regard to such published material. This is particularly offensive when we recognise the central role that disabled people and their organisations have played in the struggle for inclusion. Not one serious reference is made to the extensive publications by disabled people supporting inclusive education ... and the clear demands that disabled people have outlined with regard to their approach. Such voices are excluded from consideration. This does raise the question of whose voice is seen as significant and on what grounds? (Barton 2005, 1–2)

Recalling our observation about the indivisibility of research and activism in Barton's work, we must acknowledge that the concern with voice is in no way rhetorical. There is a meticulous concern for representation and the provision of a platform for disabled people's voices at conferences, workshops, on journal editorial and advisory boards and in faculty appointments. Of course, ensuring the presence of voice meant often-unpopular concerns for questions of access and institutional reform and flexibility.

Struggle, urgency and the challenge of writing

The 2003 professorial lecture entitled 'Inclusive Education and Teacher Education: A Basis for Hope or a Discourse of Delusion?' (Barton 2003) provides a chronicle of his thinking and writing, and of the collaborations that inspired this work. Writing with Sally Tomlinson, they were the first to apply a sustained sociological analysis to special education to expose and explore questions of power, politics and social control (Barton 2003, 3). Herein Barton and Tomlinson (1981, 1984) developed '... an approach to special education in which social interests rather than individual differences and deficits were to be a fundamental focus of analysis' (Barton 2003, 3). A 'sociological imagination' (Mills 1959) encouraged an analysis of the major policy documents and legislative acts that guided practices in special and regular education such as the 'statementing' of special educational needs and 'integration'. This form of analysis enabled them to challenge the inherently individualistic and reductionist assumptions within particular forms of psychological discourse. Their work highlighted 'assumptions concerning the significance of IQ' (Barton 2003, 3), thereby demonstrating the vulnerability of Caribbean boys and white working-class boys to low teacher expectations in schooling in England and Wales. This examination of decision-making in education laid bare the professional interest that had been clothed in discourses of benevolence and psychological defect. Accordingly, 'special educational needs' was no more than a euphemism for the inability and unwillingness of schools to educate all students (Barton 1988).

The dominant assumptions targeted comprised:

- That special education policy, provision and practice were unquestionably good for both the pupils involved and the actual system as a whole.

- That the predominant perspectives about within-the-child factors were a sufficient explanation for understanding the significant issues involved in terms of disabled pupils and children's experiences and opportunities.
- That professional decision-making was overwhelmingly in the best interests of those for whom the decisions were claimed to be made. (Barton 2003, 3)

This work, together with Tomlinson's (1981, 1982) emergent sociology of special education, represents the first application of what is now described as policy sociology to this field of study. Barton describes two powerful influences over this body of work. First was an interest in applying an alternative disciplined-based analysis to reconsider the hegemonic psychological and medical accounts of so-called special educational needs. Second was a 'quasi-Christian set of influences in which the desire was fundamentally about what I could do for and on behalf of such vulnerable and essentially dependent individuals and groups' (Barton 2003, 4).

The first of these influences – sociology – was to subject the second to profound scrutiny and develop a heightened critical reflexivity that has characterized his work in disability studies, teacher education and the sociology of education. The collaboration and friendship with disabled scholars and activists such as Mike Oliver, Colin Barnes, Jenny Morris, Vic Finkelstein, Paul Abberley, Mairian Corker and Carol Thomas (the list is obviously incomplete) invited the reconsideration of the cultures, politics and economics of education and schooling through the analytic lens of the social model of disability (UPIAS 1976; Abberley 1987; Oliver 1990; Barnes 1991; Morris 1991). Central to this work is the understanding of the way in which barriers to access and participation are formed through the unequal distribution of power according to people's impairments, illnesses and perceived differences. Disability connotes an insidious and pervasive form of oppression and exclusion from civic life rather than a scientific description of individual defectiveness and difference. The function of sociological analysis therefore becomes a means for identifying the multiplicity of oppressions in everyday life for disabled people and building cultures and practices that dismantle barriers. Barton's work in disability studies, particularly his leadership in establishing the international peer-reviewed journal *Disability and Society* (formerly *Disability, Handicap and Society*), once again exhibits a unity of research, teaching and political activism. Rejecting any form of charity derived from pity and human tragedy explanations of disablement (Oliver 1990, 1996), benevolent humanitarianism (Tomlinson 1982), Barton's work as a journal and book editor, conference organizer, teacher and mentor reflects a determination to create spaces and platforms for the voices of disabled people in the Academy. In this way he has been a major contributor to the evolution of what is referred to as insider research (Moore 2000; Titchkosky 2003).

Working with colleagues first at the University of Sheffield and later at the Institute of Education, who include Felicity Armstrong, Michele Moore, Peter Clough, Derrick Armstrong, Clare Tregaskis, Jennifer Lavia, Barbara Cole and Jenny Corbett, pioneering programmes of postgraduate studies in inclusive education spawned outstanding doctoral theses, course texts and journal manuscripts. The programmes of study and research embraced inclusive education's fundamental acknowledgement of the ubiquity of exclusion across different student identities while maintaining a central place for disability studies as an analytic and organizing focus. This work was also distinctive in its cross-cultural character and reach. Barton's work has, as many of us from 'afar' will attest, been a global conversation that welcomes voices that disrupt mono-cultural narratives. It is important to acknowledge the internationalism of Barton's work not only in text, but also in advising governments and working with disability rights organizations around the world. With his colleagues at Sheffield and the Institute of Education, Barton created expansive networks and mentored a new generation of researchers in inclusive education and disability studies in education.

Even a limited reading of the texts I have engaged with in writing this essay summons a palpable urgency in the work. For Barton there is no room for complacency. An academic life is a life of enormous privilege and responsibility. We are therefore, according to Barton, charged with a civic responsibility to contribute to the struggle against discrimination and oppression. Here we may return to the influence of a theology of liberation and deep concern for those who are marginalized and disadvantaged.

At the recent Sociology of Education Conference in London that honoured his work, Len told his colleagues of the influence of a minister who instructed him in the preparation of talks to congregations. In this way he learnt of the importance of knowing the audience, the material he was to communicate and of the necessity for passion and clarity. These lessons stayed with him, as anyone who has attended a tutorial, lecture or keynote address from Len will confirm. I mentioned Zimmerman earlier in this essay. Paths cross. At a conference I convened in Montreal, Len spoke on the morning after Bob Dylan had played at that city's famous jazz festival. To the surprise and delight of the conferees, Len commenced his talk by singing the first verse of 'The Times They Are A-Changing'. There followed a careful weaving of sociological analysis and political oration that outlined the forces of exclusion in the education marketplace and the necessity for radical interventions informed by the struggles and leadership of marginalized voices.

More shocking than a sung lecture was the revelation in an interview that writing for Len is a struggle. At one level it should not be surprising. Many of us know all too well how difficult it is to achieve accessibility without lapsing into reduction in our prose. For Barton this relates to the painful experiences of schooling, where he was pronounced a failure. This formative experience infuses passion in the words but also invites unwarranted self-doubt:

I think part of the difficulty for me has come from my earlier experiences of being in an educational context in which one was depicted as unintelligent, thick, stupid, not having abilities, so forth, and so then one actually internalizes that and one lives it out in all sorts of ways and one is extremely nervous of even putting pen to paper.[3]

Crucially important is keeping '… the human dimension present in understanding particular writings and the way in which people have presented their ideas …' (Barton 2005, 4). Ironically, in these days where the concern for accountability has become an obsession that sometimes erects bureaucratic impediments to creative productivity, impact statements should certainly dismiss this self-deprecation.

The necessity for humility as a social scientist/activist

… there's never a moment when I'm not a learner. … That … is a basis for the removing of arrogance – I detest more than ever now arrogance in the intellectual, … I cannot abide academics who give me any sense of being arrogant – there is that desire to challenge arrogance but at the same time also to challenge complacency and the recognition that these things are urgent and they are serious. (Barton 2005, 3)

While the biographer or psychologist would be tempted to scour the details of a life history to explain this deep antipathy for arrogance, it is better to consider his own reflections:

… establishing relationships with disabled people, listening to their voice and, in my case, being white, male and non-disabled, raises the following sorts of questions:

- What right have I to undertake this work?
- What responsibilities arise from the privileges I have as a result of my social position?
- How can I use my knowledge and skills to challenge forms of oppression disabled people experience?
- Does my writing and speaking reproduce a system of domination or challenge that system? (Barton 1996, 4)

It is an uncommon and refreshing event in the academy to meet someone whose interest in voice is not their own. Like so many others, my work has been challenged, enlivened and extended from reading Len's work. His questions have needled and confused me. Working through that confusion (almost) has taught me a great deal and it has been a joy and challenge to return to his early work to reconsider the impact of this work on our area of sociology in education. Writing in Harry Daniels and Philip Garner's (1999) world yearbook of education on inclusive education, Barton (1999, 54) warns of the dangers of approaching a very serious topic '... in a sterile, obtuse and dispassionate manner'. The engagement with the issues he speaks of requires the researcher to develop '... sensitive listening skills, openness, humility, and a willingness of all involved to acknowledge mistakes and/or the limitations of their own position' (Barton 1999, 54–55). His conclusion is both passionate and elegant:

> By setting the issue of disability and all forms of oppression within a human rights perspective, the possibilities for the realization of a society based on community, solidarity and in which difference can be viewed in dignified ways, becomes much stronger. (Barton 1999, 61)

In *The Culture of New Capitalism*, Richard Sennett (2006) reflects upon the 'spectre of uselessness' in new divisions of labour. It is a migratory culture where attachment to place and community are diminishing in value. Kevin McDonald (2006) coined the term 'fluidarity' as an antonym for solidarity to describe the character of social relations in this new capitalism. Bauman (2004, 39) presses us to consider the plight of surplus populations of flawed consumers. In these conditions, disadvantaged and vulnerable people are excluded. The process of exclusion is described in a seemingly objective language that blames the terms of trade, market forces, efficiency requirements, and economic downturns (Bauman 2004, 40). In truth the actors in this drama are real people with names and addresses (Bauman 2004, 40). Barton and his colleagues have, over the years, applied this very human face to the sociology of education. In particular, they have applied it to the ways in which attempts have been made through medicine, psychology and theories of education administration to obscure the deeply political activity of calibrating, categorizing and excluding students through diagnoses and treatments of so-called special educational needs.

Acknowledgements
The author is grateful to colleagues Felicity Armstrong and Michele Moore for reading and commenting upon this essay. The author would also like to thank the reviewers for their very helpful suggestions.

Notes
1. Here I refer to the deliberate strategy of inviting speakers representing a range of theoretical positions to grapple with serious social issues.
2. Representative key figures in the development of the sociology of education in the UK.
3. From an unpublished transcript of an interview with Professor Barton in Montreal, April 11, 2005. The interview was conducted by Julie Allan and Roger Slee.

References
Abberley, P. 1987. The concept of oppression and the development of a social theory of disability. *Disability, Handicap & Society* 2, no. 1: 5–19.

Allan, J., and R. Slee. 2008. *Doing inclusive education research.* Rotterdam: Sense Publishers.

Barnes, C. 1991. *Disabled people in Britain and discrimination: A case for anti-discrimination legislation.* London: Hurst in association with the British Council of Organizations of Disabled People.

Barton, L. 1988. *The politics of special educational needs.* London: Falmer.

Barton, L., ed. 1996. *Disability and society: Emerging issues and insights.* London: Longman.

Barton, L. 1998. Developing an emancipatory research agenda: Possibilities and dilemmas. In *Articulating with difficulty: Research voices in inclusive education,* ed. P. Clough and L. Barton, 29–39. London: Paul Chapman Publishing.

Barton, L. 1999. Market ideologies, education and the challenge for inclusion. In *Inclusive education: Supporting inclusion in education systems,* ed. H. Daniels and P. Garner, 54–62. London: Kogan Page.

Barton, L. 2003. Inclusive education and teacher education: A basis for hope or a discourse of delusion? Professorial lecture, Institute of Education, London.

Barton, L. 2005. Special educational needs: An alternative look. A response to Warnock M. 2005. Special educational needs – a new look. http://www.leeds.ac.uk/disability-studies/archiveuk/barton/Warnock.pdf (accessed November 18, 2009).

Barton, L., and M. Oliver, eds. 1997. *Disability studies: Past, present and future.* Leeds: The Disability Press.

Barton, L., and S. Tomlinson, eds. 1981. *Special education: Policy, practices and social issues.* London: Harper & Row.

Barton, L., and S. Tomlinson, eds. 1984. *Special education and social interests.* London: Croom Helm.

Bauman, Z. 2004. *Wasted lives: Modernity and its outcasts.* Oxford: Polity.

Clough, P., and L. Barton, eds. 1998. *Articulating with difficulty: Research voices in inclusive education.* London: Paul Chapman Publishing.

Connell, R. 1993. *Schools and social justice.* Philadelphia, PA: Temple University Press.

Corbett, J. 1998. 'Voice' in emancipatory research: Imaginative listening. In *Articulating with difficulty,* ed. P. Clough and L. Barton, 54–63. London: Paul Chapman Publishing.

Daniels, H., and P. Garner. 1999. *Inclusive education: Supporting inclusion in education systems.* London: Kogan Page.

Foster, P., R. Gomm, and M. Hammersley. 1996. *Constructing educational inequality: An assessment of research on school processes.* London: Falmer Press.

Freire, P. 1972. *Pedagogy of the oppressed.* Harmondsworth: Penguin.

Hammersley, M. 2000. *Taking sides in social research: Essays on partisanship and bias.* London: Routledge.

McDonald, K. 2006. *Global movements: Action and culture.* Oxford: Blackwell.

Mills, C.M. 1959. *The sociological imagination.* New York: Oxford University Press.

Moore, M., ed. 2000. *Insider perspectives on inclusion: Raising voices, raising issues.* Sheffield: Philip Armstrong.

Morris, J. 1991. *Pride against prejudice: Personal politics of disability.* London: Women's Press.

Oliver, M. 1990. *The politics of disablement.* London: Macmillan Education.

Oliver, M. 1992. Changing the social relations of research production? *Disability, Handicap & Society* 7, no. 2: 101–14.

Oliver, M. 1996. *Understanding disability: From theory to practice.* Basingstoke: Macmillan.

Sennett, R. 2006. *The culture of the new capitalism.* New Haven, CT: Yale University Press.

Titchkosky, T. 2003. *Disability, self, and society.* Toronto: University of Toronto Press.

Tomlinson, S. 1981. *Educational subnormality: A study in decision-making.* London: Routledge & Kegan Paul.

Tomlinson, S. 1982. *A sociology of special education.* London: Routledge & Kegan Paul.

Troyna, B. 1994. Blind faith? Empowerment and educational research. *International Studies in Sociology of Education* 4, no. 1: 3–24.

UPIAS. 1976. Fundamental principles of disability. Report for Union of the Physically Impaired Against Segregation, London.

Vygotsky, L.S. 1962. *Thought and language.* Cambridge, MA: MIT Press.

Warnock, M. 2005. *Special educational needs: A new look.* Keele: Philosophy of Education Society of Great Britain.

Lessons for higher education: the university as a site of activism

Kathleen Lynch

UCD Equality Studies Centre, UCD School of Social Justice, University College Dublin, Dublin, Ireland

Len Barton is acutely aware of the power of the academy to either enhance critical thinking or to depress it. He is a true academic, never accepting the received wisdom or perspective of any given sociological standpoint, no matter how powerful or fashionable it was at the time. He has encouraged and promoted a unique blend of professional and public sociology of education that has left a profound legacy not only in the United Kingdom but beyond. While the neo-liberal ideology had hegemonic status for most of his professional life, Len chose to engage in a counter-ideological struggle; he created new intellectual spaces in the academy where people could safely dissent from the reigning intellectual orthodoxies. He operated according to the principles of Gramscian thinking by mounting a war of position, in journals, books, teaching, conferences and research, for critical intellectuals. And he encouraged other people to do likewise. This article explores the ways in which Len's work inspired the establishment of the Equality Studies Centre and the School of Social Justice in University College Dublin. It outlines the lessons learned from Len Barton about higher education and its potential as a site for critical analysis and action.

Introduction

Len Barton is an engaged sociologist, a critical organic intellectual of humanity at large; he is not confined in his intellectual allegiances or interests, but seeks to bring the voices from the margins to the academy in a researched and organised fashion. He is a universalistic rather than a particularistic sociologist. This is reflected in the way he encourages and promotes all forms of critical research and teaching, especially those that were focused on social justice issues. He is a pioneer in mainstreaming research with disabled people in education, by no means a fashionable subject for sociologists in the 1980s.

While there is much to learn from Len's scholarship, there are also lessons to learn for organising resistance in higher education from the way he created

47

and protected spaces for dissenting voices. In this article I give an account of how Len's work played an important role in enabling us to establish and maintain the Equality Studies Centre in University College Dublin (UCD) as a site of critical education, research and academic activism for 20 years, a movement that led to establishing the School of Social Justice in 2005 when Equality Studies and Women's Studies worked together to form a new school in the university. The paper analyses the dynamics of the academic movement and the role Len played in helping to secure it.

The academic legacy

Len has played a major role in the promotion of sociology of education and disability studies at a time when critical thinking within all sociological frames has been under attack. He has not taken the easy route of scientific formalism that flourished in so many sociology fields from the 1970s onwards (Calhoun 2005). He eschewed those branches of the discipline that guaranteed 'careers', where trivial findings were given status at the expense of innovative reframing of sociological questions. He has always been critical, always asking new questions, and refusing to accept received wisdoms no matter how much they accorded with his own political and intellectual perspectives. His ability to keep on asking awkward questions, to remain forever sceptical of certainty in science, meant that he has never rested intellectually. He has had no clearly defined academic comfort-zone, and it was this critical legacy that makes Len such an important scholar within the social sciences of disability studies and sociology of education.

Len also epitomises the reflexive sociological voice. His ability to look beyond what was presented, to ask the missing question, to name the missing presence, to constantly query whatever orthodoxy was at hand, has made him an invaluable academic colleague. He is not representative of sectional interests, even those within the disability movement. He retained a critical distance from all forms of institutional power, including those aligned with social movements with which he was intellectually associated (Barton 1988). Through his work he has created a space for all types of sociology to flourish, be it professional, critical, public or policy-oriented (Burawoy 2005). He did this very effectively within the fields of education and disability studies.

A third way in which Len contributed significantly to academic life has been through his work on research design and methodology. He did not simply do 'transformative or emancipatory research' as some type of add-on to academic analysis (Barton 2005). He has been intrinsically emancipatory and enabling in his approach to all forms of scholarship. He facilitated a dialogue between experiential knowledge and academic propositional knowledge, especially in the journal *Disability and Society* that has had a profound and lasting effect on the way research is undertaken with disabled people. Through this journal, and other publications, he helped bring an end to the colonisation of disability as a research issue by those who had no interest in challenging injustices of recognition, power and resources that have plagued disabled people as research 'subjects' (Barton 1988, 1989a, 1989b, 2001). He has played a major role in democratising the relations of research production, distribution and exchange in the disability field.

No tribute to Len that focused solely on his scholarship would be complete without reference to the way ethics and integrity has been integrated into his academic work. Len has brought a level of honesty to research and theory in education that is thoroughly refreshing. He did not seek out the powerful scholars across different countries that would advance his own profile in the new academic capitalist order (Slaughter and Leslie 2001). Rather, he sought to support those critical and engaged scholars who were struggling to survive, swimming against the tide of new right politics and policies in the post-1990s era across a range of countries. Through the conferences and journals he developed, he created intellectual spaces for critical thinkers like Peter Mayo and Mary Darmanin in Malta, Helen Phtiaka in Cyprus and Xavier Rambla in Catalonia. Len also created an important international network for critical sociologists of education in Ireland.

The impact of Len's work

I first met Len Barton in the mid-1980s when I attended the Sociology of Education Conference that he convened annually in Westhill College in Birmingham. I had read Len's co-edited works *Schooling, Ideology and Curriculum* (Barton, Meighan, and Walker 1980) and *Gender, Class and Education* (Walker and Barton 1983) and I was looking for a sociological pathway that would guide me along the road to praxis, integrating academic work with activism. Being an activist as well as an academic, I never felt quite at ease with the certainties of university theorising about inequality, especially where this theorising was far removed from the sources of injustices that generated it. I saw Len as a kindred spirit in this regard. He had a deep and profound understanding of Gouldner's (1970) thesis, namely that the domain assumptions arising from our own biography impact on our paradigmatic assumptions. He has always been sensitive to the positionality of the theorist, to the fact that there is no view from nowhere in sociological terms.

In the 1980s, my experience of sociological research was that of a discipline that was working increasingly at a comfortable distance from those who had experiential knowledge of injustice. When social scientists wrote about inequality, their upper-middle-class domain assumptions seemed to dictate their paradigmatic proclamations about injustice (Lynch and O'Neill 1994). Their personal and professional positionality seemed to remove them from the urgency and injuries of the injustices they documented (Oliver 1992; Reay 2000; Adair 2005). Academic sociologists were trained to write about 'the poor', 'the disabled', 'women' or other oppressed groups without recognising the colonising character of research relations. They wrote about the oppressed as if they knew them better than they knew themselves; they often stole their voice and spoke in their name without seeing or knowing how demeaning and oppressive this act could be.

The way sociologists were working as professional commentators on inequality was epitomised for me in the work undertaken by social stratification theorists who saw social mobility as the pinnacle of egalitarian advancement (Goldthorpe 1980). The deep-seated inegalitarian premise underpinning this classical liberal view of 'equality-as-social mobility' was almost impossible to challenge; mobility was the liberal equality mantra and to question it was to challenge the hegemonic voices of the sociological elite. Len has been instrumental in breaking up that hegemony, not only by challenging the simple equal opportunities model that was so dominant in all areas of education (Barton, Meighan, and Walker 1980; Walker and Barton 1983) but by highlighting the multiple forms that inequality could take, not least by focusing on disability and related exclusions over time (Barton and Moody 1981; Barton and Oliver 1992; Armstrong, Armstrong, and Barton 2000).

Len's work has that sense of urgency and outrage that asks you to do more than simply become intellectually engaged with the subject matter at hand. While he expected excellence in scholarship (before 'excellence' became simply a marketing strategy), he also expected engagement and equality of respect and recognition for those who were defined as the 'subjects' of research. He has been committed to transforming research relations in the disability area and the relations between those professionals who offered educational services and those who were recipients (Barton 1988).

The conferences organised annually by Len became almost a place of pilgrimage, a source of inspiration and hope. They were a lifeline for people who were relatively isolated intellectually and politically in their work. He gave academic dissidents like myself an academic community to call in on, one that also supported and challenged simultaneously. No matter how much Len respected what you did, he always asked you to move on intellectually, to address other questions, take on new perspectives, to know that there is no resting place for engaged academics.

Len's influence on my work was not confined to what I learned from the conferences he organised. I also learned greatly from his writing, challenging the ideological underpinnings of special needs education (Barton 1986, 1988, 1989a, 1989b, 2001; Barton and Oliver 1992). While I had always had a deep suspicion of the ideological biases inherent in the concept of 'general intelligence', developed from the time I had worked in a research centre engaged in test development, it was Len's work that galvanised my critique (Lynch 1999). And that had implications for how we developed our relationship in Equality Studies with disabled people in Ireland.

Impact on Ireland

At the time that Len was challenging disablism in education in his early work, Ireland was still firmly working within a medical model; there was almost no dissent. We invited Len and he gave a lecture in April 1992 entitled 'Disability: The Necessity of a Socio-political Perspective'. As this lecture was attended by key figures in the disability movement and funded by the National Rehabilitation Board (the State agency managing the disability sector at the time), it played an important role in opening up a new debate about disability. With Len's help and support we subsequently invited his academic collaborators, including Mike Oliver, Sally French and Colin Barnes, to give lectures over a five-year period from 1993 to 1997 inclusive. As this was a time of transition in Irish politics, when the equality legislation was being planned, the lectures were of considerable importance in policy terms. They helped introduce a new language to the disability movement in Ireland, fore-fronting equal rights and respect for disabled people, making a space for them to name their own injustices. They played an important role in moving the policy framework from one based on charity to one based on principles of equality for disabled people. The dividend from Len's work is found in the acceptance, at government level, of an equality-based discourse epitomised in the 1996 report of the Commission on the Status of People with Disabilities (Government of Ireland 1996). While the gains from that time have been rolled back in new legislation in the mid-2000s that did not endorse rights-based claims to services (de Wispelaere and Walsh 2007), nonetheless the rights of disabled people not to experience discrimination in employment and in accessing services have been enshrined in a formal way in the Employment Equality Act (1998) and in the Equal Status Act (2000).

The public interest role of the university

From an academic perspective, one of Len's greatest achievements, in my view, has been the way he has envisioned the role of the researcher and the academy in social life. His profound understanding of how the academy should and could work in the public interest is one of his greatest legacies.

Len has a deep sociological understanding of the politics of higher education. He saw how universities were being transformed increasingly into powerful consumer-oriented corporate networks, whose public interest values were seriously challenged (Davies, Gottsche, and Bansel 2006; Rutherford 2005). Although higher education *per se* was not his primary research subject, he recognised that commercialisation had been normalised and granted moral legitimacy (Giroux 2002), and that its operational values and purposes have been encoded in the systems of all types of universities (Dill and Soo 2005; Steier 2003). Moreover, his move to create new safe intellectual spaces for critical thought showed that he recognised that both the pace and intensity of commercialisation had been exacerbated (Bok 2003; Henkel 1997). Yet Len was committed to the vision of universities as public interest institutions. Like Harkavy (2006), he did not believe that one could pretend that there was no difference between the commercial and public interests. And he also realised that to serve public interest values in higher education would be a struggle. In this context he became a great supporter of our work in UCD, helping us to maintain Equality Studies and develop the School of Social Justice as intellectual spaces built on the Freirean notion of critically engaged scholarship and praxis (Lynch, Crean, and Moran 2009).

Academics are granted the freedom from necessity to write and to teach in the public interest; however, there is a choice whether or not to use that freedom to act. While Len engaged in teaching, researching and publishing to promote critical thinking, he used his academic freedom in a way that most do not, by institutionalising journals and ways of doing research and teaching that will last over time. In particular he gave voice to people and issues that had been ignored in academia, most memorably the voice of disabled people in *Disability and Society*. But he has also made space for those who believed that the quality of education mattered at all levels, including higher education, by establishing *Teaching in Higher Education*. He has created a forum for debate for those committed to critical excellence in sociology of education by founding the *British Journal of Sociology of Education* and *International Studies in Sociology of Education*.

What Len also did, and what many may not know, is that he created safe spaces for many new and lesser known academics from small places and countries by encouraging them to publish in the journals that he founded. For those who live in the academic metropole, the intellectual perspective of those on the periphery is not generally of much interest (Alatas 2003; Connell 2007). Although Len has been at the centre of the metropole, in the sense that he was situated in powerful universities in a major power stronghold of English-speaking academic publishing in the United Kingdom, he has always been reflexive and conscious of his own power and the potential it had to exclude or include those on the margins. While he did not write about this, his actions spoke to his principles. He made a deliberate attempt to include those who were on the margins of the metropole, particularly welcoming scholars who were marginalised in their own countries and communities due to their critical academic standpoint. I felt I belonged in both categories, as indeed did other Irish scholars that Len supported, including Patrick McDonnell, who has played a pioneering role in challenging the medical model of disability and in recognising the linguistic and cultural uniqueness of the Deaf community (McDonnell 2007). Len was also supportive of new scholars like Dympna Devine who promoted an innovative children's rights perspective in education and public life in Ireland (Devine 2003). When one examined the list of invitees to the sociology of education conferences organised by Len each year, not only did the list include 'big names' in sociology of education, it also included academics from a wide range of smaller European Union states. The wide range of people involved in contributing chapters to the many books that he edited also reflected his breadth of understanding of how the politics of knowledge worked and how to set agendas by recognising dissident voices (Barton and Tomlinson 1981; Arnot and Barton 1992; Armstrong, Armstrong, and Barton 2000).

Len has played a quiet but important role in both encouraging and supporting us to set up and maintain the UCD Equality Studies Centre in 1990, and to establish the UCD School of Social Justice in 2005. While he has not been our sole supporter,[1] his belief in the mission we had set ourselves, to educate social justice and egalitarian-led activists from all walks of life, was profoundly reassuring over years of struggle for survival (Lynch 1995; Lynch, Crean, and Moran 2009).

With the postmodernist turn and the rise of neo-liberal politics, it seemed intellectually vagrant and academically suicidal to establish a Centre for Equality Studies in UCD in the late 1980s. Yet it was precisely these challenges that inspired us to act. And it was my visits to the conferences that Len organised every New Year (I never liked the timing, in early January, but I knew I would be reinvigorated when I returned!) that reassured us the educational work we were doing was worthwhile. In particular it reassured me that the approach which we took to our work was appropriate in our context. We learned from Len that while the scientific, including the sociological, must be distinguished from the political (Martinelli 2008), there is a need to allow spaces for more than professional sociology or policy sociology (or the professional and policy-led dimensions of any disciplines) to thrive (Burawoy 2005). Arising from his own work with disabled activists and academics, he encouraged us to protect the spaces for the sub-altern within disciplines (Barton and Oliver 1992). He recognised that there must be a space for academic knowledge to learn from experiential knowledge, with its complex positive and normative dimensions, especially in the study of injustices.

Questioning the binary between positive/normative has long been a key issue for us in Equality Studies (Baker et al. 2004). Len respected this position. Like Andrew Sayer (2006), he recognised that much research in the social sciences is profoundly unitary in terms of the normative and the positive. Even for those who do not subscribe to critical perspectives, and lay claim to independence, the normative is encoded in every publication and every lecture. When scholars write of 'discrimination' in law, 'exploitation' in sociology or 'marginalisation' in education, they are not just describing a phenomenon, they are also naming it as undesirable because it undermines the well-being of particular groups of people. They are making a normative judgement as well as an empirical statement, even if they do not explicitly name their normative position.

Len has long recognised that taking a 'critical' approach to scholarship promotes a particular normative position and set of values that makes the very critique of oppression, and indeed the enterprise of much academic work, meaningful. While objectivity is vital for scientific analysis and for choosing the appropriate instruments for research investigation, there is an implicit normative dimension to the knowledge act.

Equality studies and social justice – keeping a place in the university

'If you want to interrupt the right, study what they themselves did' (Apple 2007, 168). While the setting up of Equality Studies, and of the School of Social Justice, was inspired by a Gramscian-informed understanding of the role of culture and ideology in the realisation of change, and by the Freirean recognition of education's lack of neutrality, it was also inspired by lessons learned from the success of Thatcherism in the United Kingdom, and by the response to Thatcher's attacks on sociology by people like Len. One of the major achievements of the Thatcher era was that not only did it change the terms of political discourse in the United Kingdom, it successfully institution-alised neo-liberal beliefs and values in law and public policy. Len chose to engage in a counter-ideological struggle; he was directly involved in challeng-ing the academic ideologues of the conservatives and neo-liberals by provid-ing spaces in the academy. He operated according to the principles of Gramscian thinking in terms of challenging hegemonic ideologies, mounting a war of position in journals, teaching, conferences and research for critical intellectuals (Gramsci 1971).

While writing and teaching is the tool of the academic who wants to act for global justice, there is a need as Harkavy (2006, 7) has observed for 'strategic organisational innovation'. There is a need to institutionalise ideals in the structures of organisations not just in their language or written policies, no matter how essential the latter may be. One of the reasons inequalities are often difficult to challenge is because they are institutionalised in the catego-ries of everyday life (Tilly 1998). By the same logic, if egalitarian changes are to be instituted, they need to be institutionalised in categories, positions, processes and systems that are built on egalitarian and social justice principles. Len understood the primacy of building institutions that would outlive their incumbents and the importance of 'strategic organisational innovation'. Len encouraged us (as did many other supporting academics inside and outside Ireland) in Equality Studies, and subsequently in the School of Social Justice, to institutionalise a physical and intellectual space to promote research and teaching on equality and social justice. We learned from what Len had achieved at his conferences, and through the journals he established and his publications, that while it was necessary to have programmes of education and research in the short term, in the medium to long term it was necessary to have an institutional base to help secure the future for critical thought and practice.

In realising change, there is a need to identify the interstices that Habermas noted, those places between spaces that allow for change and resistances to occur at different times. Times of transition within institutions are times that offer opportunities for resistance, for finding spaces to create new initiatives.

While times of transition are also times of social closure, re-regulation and control, when those in power set out the terms of change and try to control its scope and impact, the transition itself creates instabilities. New orders are created and spaces are opened up to establish new programmes and initiatives if there are the resources to fight for these at the time. There is a very real sense in which these times of transition involve what Gramsci defined as 'wars of position'.

While Len used the cracks in Thatcher's academies to create new discourses of disability and inclusion, and new institutions to support these in the forms of books, journal and conferences, we used the uncertainty of transitions, in 1990 and 2004/05, to both initiate Equality Studies and to propose changes in courses, programmes and activities in the university.[2] At each time, the proposals were met with oppositions, counter-resistances; not necessarily from central management, who were less concerned with their ideologies than with their likelihood of success, but by colleagues in other departments and schools, sometimes for ideological reasons (dislike of all things critical or socially engaged) and sometimes for fear that the programmes we offered might jeopardise their own subject or department. There is a lengthy correspondence in our files and emails on these challenges; having a team of colleagues who were committed to the project, and supporting academic colleagues, from inside and outside Ireland, who had a clear vision as to our role and purpose was crucial. It should also be noted, and Len appreciated and encouraged this, that our continuance was also greatly assisted by critically engaged civil society organisations that wanted us to promote the education of their own activists.

Institutional change offers threats as well as opportunities and these have also to be managed. In 2005, 'restructuring' was the euphemism for closing down unwanted departments in universities. It was the neo-liberal gospel for higher education in Ireland, promulgated by the OECD in 2004 under the guise of an 'independent review'. As with almost all centres, Equality Studies was threatened with closure, or its surrogate, amalgamation into a larger 'established discipline'. We refused to accept this, and demonstrated that the Equality Studies Centre was a 'brand name' (using the market rhetoric of the new regime) and necessary for the survival of our work. We also used data we had accumulated (ironically, due to accountability demands over the years) to demonstrate our ability to set up a school. We knew that we had to get 'school' status if we were to survive, as schools were going to have legal status under the new statutes of the university. It would be more difficult to disestablish a school than a programme of studies or a centre because of its institutionalised standing.[3] In 2005 we established the School of Social Justice, where Women's Studies and Equality Studies are partners. Knowing that we had the support of people like Len at this time (and indeed in earlier times) was crucial; not because he was asked to act, but because we know he would if called upon.

Challenges – disciplinary issues

Our affinity with Len, and with the people in Disability Studies in the University of Leeds to whom we were introduced by Len, showed us that Equality Studies experienced the same difficulties that Disability Studies and all interdisciplinary fields including Women's Studies experience; it was and is not seen to be 'pure' scholarship; it is tainted by diversity[4] and tolerated on the boundaries of the academy (O'Connor 2006). Although there is recognition internationally of the central importance of interdisciplinary and transdisciplinary research (Nowotny, Scott, and Gibbons 2001), there is little status attached to such new areas of scholarship in most established universities.[5] Fields of study are indeed allowed to emerge but the core activities of the university centre around 'established disciplines'. The history of our experience in this respect is salutary.

The established faculties of UCD (which were assimilated into colleges in 2005) did not regard interdisciplinary programmes as 'pure' enough in academic terms to house them when they were first established, so Equality Studies (and other similar 'studies' including Disability Studies and Women's Studies) was faculty-homeless for several years until an Interdisciplinary Faculty was established in 2003. When, in the autumn of 2004, the new president and his 'team' began to 'rationalise' (a euphemism for close down) a number of faculties and departments, the Interdisciplinary Faculty to which we belonged was closed and Equality Studies was relocated to the College of Human Sciences. In all, over 90 departments in the university were reduced to 35 departments and renamed as 'schools'.[6] There was considerable pressure on Equality Studies to join established single-discipline schools at this time. The likelihood that we would be minor players in large and otherwise mono-disciplinary schools (and our knowledge of what had happened to Cultural Studies in Birmingham University when they had been amalgamated; Rutherford 2005) motivated us to push for the establishment of a new interdisciplinary institutional space within the new university structures, in the form of the School of Social Justice. This idea was accepted in principle after making a strong written case to the President as to the importance of social justice in the history and future of the university, and fighting for the school at numerous board and faculty meetings. In addition, we used the university's own ideology, which promotes the idea that UCD works for the entire community, to challenge our closure;[7] it was an exercise in legitimation (Thompson 1990). However, Women's Studies was the only centre that agreed to join the new School of Social Justice. The Disability Studies Centre joined Psychology and The Development Studies Centre joined Politics, although we had asked them to join Social Justice.[8] In each case, the titles of the new schools did not reflect the merger, a further indication of the institutional hostility to interdisciplinarity. Politics was renamed as the School of Politics, and International Relations and Psychology retained its name with no mention of Disability Studies.

In the neo-liberal age, fear plays a major role in controlling and regulating academic staff (Boden and Epstein 2006). Moreover, because academics are taken over on a daily basis with anxieties about productivity within an intense system of surveillance, they disavow their own docility (Davies, Gottsche, and Bansel 2006). And fear was a major reason why academic staff did not want to join Social Justice; not just because it was seen to be a school without an 'established' disciplinary centre, but because colleagues believed that such a school would be closed down in time. However, fear was not the only motivation. Some of those we invited to join us made it clear that they did not wish to be part of a school based on the principle of social justice. The division between the normative and the positive was a priority value in the minds of many colleagues; Equality Studies and Social Justice had broken a taboo by aligning the normative and the positive, and this continued to be unacceptable.[9]

Challenges – academic capitalism

While academic life has always been highly individualised and driven by personal interests and ambitions, it was not always as driven by academic capitalism as it is currently (Slaughter and Rhoades 2004). Len always appreciated how even not-for-profit higher education programmes had been forced to be a domain of market activity in recent years. He recognised how, under the globalised (and highly unscientific) league table regimes promoted by commercial interests, universities could not determine the conditions of their own appraisal (Marginson 2006). Educational programmes that service low-income communities, or research that is of value at national level, do not feature on university rankings. And as the experience of Cultural Studies in Birmingham (Rutherford 2005) and multidisciplinary programmes and Women's Studies in many countries show, what is not counted can be closed. There is a serious threat to critical thought posed by marketised higher educational systems (Webster 2004); it is a challenge Equality Studies has to confront. However, history is there to be made, it is not pre-given. Len has been one of the key people who reminded us of how being aware of the dangers and challenges facing the project is a key factor in survival and progression

Facing up to regulation and counting

Like Disability Studies and Women's Studies, by definition, the Equality Studies Centre and the School of Social Justice have to be socially engaged. Their work has a public dimension, in terms of researching with and educating those who work in social movements for social justice. Yet, if academic productivity is being measured by a narrowly construed bibliometric measure, public service engagement with vulnerable civil society groups is precluded. It simply does not count up as value in journal rankings. The devaluing of dialogue with persons and bodies other than academics effectively privatises learning among those who are paid-up members of the academic community, be it as students or academics. The lack of dialogue with civil social-justice-oriented groups in society in particular also forecloses the opportunity to have equality hypotheses tested or challenged from an experiential standpoint. It limits the opportunities for learning that occur when there is a dialogue between experiential and theoretical knowledge of injustice.

There is a strange irony in a narrowly framed peer review system, focused on bibliometric measurement that currently underpins the reward system of academic life. It encourages the 'good' academic to be detached, to become silent in the public sphere by dialoguing only with academic peers, ideally in international peer-reviewed journals rather than books. The disincentive to engage in public dialogue is also a product of the positive/normative binary, and the pressure on academics to eschew normative values if they are to demonstrate their credibility as legitimate scientists. Challenging the silencing is part of the struggle. And Len has shown ways of doing this, particularly in the journal *Disability and Society*, where the voices of activists and academics are presented singly and/or together. It is a very practical example of institutionalised critically engaged scholarship in the making. It enables one to be both inside and outside the academy simultaneously.

Conclusion

Universities and higher education institutions are not neutral agents in the field of academic discourse. Like all educational institutions, they work either for 'domestication or for freedom' (Freire 1972). Universities are projects in the making, places in which academics can either become agents of history or docile subjects (Davies, Gottsche, and Bansel 2006).

What Len's academic life and work shows is that rather than being bewildered and overwhelmed by neo-capitalist academic rhetoric, we need to re-envisage and re-invent the university as a place of scholarly work grounded in the principles of democracy, equality and care that are at the heart of the public education tradition. And we need to re-emerge from the careerism and docility that is so much a feature of the neo-liberal university to do this (Davies, Gottsche, and Bansel 2006). All of this means that we must reassess our position as critical intellectuals, and face-up to the limitations of the positive-normative divide (Sayer 2006), especially in the analysis of injustices.

Just as Len has done, we must also allow space for the sub-altern to emerge both across and within disciplines so that the professional aspects of disciplines do not blind us to the need for engagement with the most significant issues of our time (Burawoy 2005). Creating space in the university for scholarship on equality and social justice demands a dialogue with experiential knowledge holders. As Len's work in disability studies shows, those with experiential knowledge of injustice have much to teach us as theorists and researchers; and through education and research the university can in turn re-resource activists. Having a dialogue means democratising the social relations of teaching, learning, and exchange. Institutionalising ways of enabling the sub-altern to speak back has been one of Len's major contributions to sociology and to disability studies; there are few academics that have such credits to their name.

Notes

1. There are many, many academics from different countries who have supported us in developing and maintaining Equality Studies over the years; they could not all be listed here. However, we are especially grateful to Madelene Arnot, Michael Apple, Colin Barnes, Diane Reay, Andrew Sayer and Erik Olin Wright for their sustained support over many years.
2. We proposed new courses and programmes: an MSc and Graduate Diploma in Equality Studies, in the late 1980s and 1990, which naturally evolved to a PhD programme. We established a Certificate programme in 1994, and undergraduate optional courses in 2005, available to all university students. We also devised new structures as we worked: a working group in 1987, a centre in 1990 and a new research and teaching network in 2005 – the Egalitarian World Initiative 2005 (www.ucd.ie/esc, www.ucd.ie/ewi).
3. Equality Studies led the movement to create the School of Social Justice in 2005 with the support of Women's Studies. Although the School of Social Justice is one of the 35 statutorily recognised schools within new statutes of the university, this does not mean that Equality Studies and the school are institutionally unassailable. There will be new transitions to be managed in the future.
4. There are four full-time permanent academics and one permanent researcher in Equality Studies representing five different fields of study: economics, education, law, political philosophy, and sociology. There is also a part-time permanent post held by the Outreach Co-ordinator who runs the Certificate (non-graduate programme), and a range of researchers and post-doctoral fellows whose positions are funded by research grants.
5. At a college meeting in spring 2008, the vice-president for research at UCD (who had a medical background) referred to the non-traditional subjects in the university as those offering 'funny degrees'.
6. The change in nomenclature from faculties to 'colleges' and departments to 'schools' was not merely symbolic; it heralded a whole new set of power relations wherein responsibility was devolved to schools and colleges, and power was centralised in the so-called Senior Management Team of the presidents, vice-presidents, heads of the five colleges and other co-optees. The changes were institutionalised in new university statutes.
7. The UCD logo is '*Ad Astra Cothromh Féinne*', which means literally 'Reaching for excellence (the stars) and working for the entire community'.
8. While a few individual staff from former centres and departments did want to join Social Justice, they were strongly encouraged by the university to accept the majority decision.
9. The place where this was forcibly articulated was at a meeting two colleagues and I were called to attend on 19 July 2005. The meeting was called on the pretext that it was to help us work out a framework for developing the Egalitarian World Initiative Network (www.ucd.ie/ewi) within the College of Human Sciences. It turned out to be an *ad hoc* meeting, attended by four senior professors and a few other

college staff; it was made clear to us that they were opposed to the work we were doing in the Egalitarian World Initiative and the new School of Social Justice. We were told we were 'politicising the university' and 'bringing it into disrepute'.

References

Adair, V. 2005. US working class/poverty-class divides. *Sociology* 39, no. 5: 817–34.

Alatas, F. 2003. Academic dependency and colonisation in the social sciences. *Current Sociology* 51, no. 6: 599–613.

Apple, M. 2007. Social movements and political practice in education. *Theory and Research in Education* 5, no. 2: 161–71.

Armstrong, F., D. Armstrong, and L. Barton, eds. 2000. *Inclusive education: Policy, contexts and comparative perspectives.* London: D. Fulton.

Arnot, M., and L. Barton, eds. 1992. *Voicing concerns: Sociological perspectives on contemporary education reforms.* Wallingford: Triangle Books.

Baker, J., K. Lynch, S. Cantillon, and J. Walsh. 2004. *Equality: From theory to action.* London: Palgrave Macmillan.

Barton, L. 1986. The politics of special educational needs. *Disability, Handicap & Society* 1, no. 3: 273–90.

Barton, L., ed. 1988. *The politics of special educational needs.* Lewes: The Falmer Press.

Barton, L., ed. 1989a. *Disability and dependency.* Lewes: Falmer Press.

Barton, L., ed. 1989b. *Integration: Myth or reality?* Lewes: Falmer Press.

Barton, L., ed. 2001. *Disability, politics and the struggle for change.* London: David Fulton.

Barton, L. 2005. Emancipatory research and disabled people: Some observations and questions. *Educational review* 57, no. 3: 317–27.

Barton, L., and S. Moody. 1981. The value of parents to the ESN(s) school: An examination. In *Special education: Policy, practices and social issues,* ed. L. Barton and S. Tomlinson, 133–48. London: Harper and Row.

Barton, L., and M. Oliver. 1992. Special needs: Personal trouble or public issue. In *Voicing concerns: Sociological perspectives on contemporary educational reforms,* ed. M. Arnot and L. Barton, 66–87. Wallingford: Triangle Books.

Barton, L., R. Meighan, and S. Walker, eds. 1980. *Schooling, ideology and the curriculum.* Politics and Education Series. Lewes: The Falmer Press.

Barton, L., and S. Tomlinson, eds. 1981. *Special education: Policy, practices and issues.* London: Harper and Row.

Boden, R., and D. Epstein. 2006. Managing the research imagination? Globalisation and research in higher education. *Globalisation, Societies and Education* 4, no. 2: 223–36.

Bok, D. 2003. *Universities in the marketplace: The commercialization of higher education.* Princeton, NJ: Princeton University Press.

Burawoy, M. 2005. 2004 American Sociological Association Presidential Address: For public sociology. *British Journal of Sociology* 56, no. 2: 259–94.

Calhoun, C. 2005. The promise of public sociology. *British Journal of Sociology* 56, no. 3: 355–63.

Connell, R.W. 2007. *Southern theory: The global dynamics of knowledge in social science.* Cambridge: Polity Press.

Davies, B., M. Gottsche, and P. Bansel. 2006. The rise and fall of the neo-liberal university. *European Journal of Education* 41, no. 2: 305–19.

Devine, D. 2003. *Children, power and schooling*. Stoke-on-Trent: Trentham Books.

de Wispelaere, J., and J. Walsh. 2007. Disability rights in Ireland: Chronicle of a missed opportunity. *Irish Political Studies* 22, no. 4: 517–43.

Dill, D.D., and M. Soo. 2005. Academic quality, league tables and public policy: A cross national analysis of university ranking systems. *Higher Education* 49: 495–533.

Freire, P. 1972. *Pedagogy of the oppressed*. London: Penguin.

Giroux, H. 2002. Neoliberalism, corporate culture and the promise of higher education: The university as a democratic public sphere. *Harvard Educational Review* 72, no. 4: 1–31.

Goldthorpe, J. 1980. *Social mobility and class structure in modern Britain*. Oxford: Clarendon Press.

Gouldner, A.W. 1970. *The coming crisis of western sociology*. London: H.E.B. Heinmann.

Government of Ireland. 1996. *A strategy for equality: Report of the Commission on the Status of People with Disabilities*. Dublin: Government Publications Office.

Gramsci, A. 1971. *Selections from the prison notebooks of Antonio Gramsci*. Ed. and trans. Q. Hoare and G. Nowell Smith. London: Lawrence and Wishart.

Harkavy, I. 2006. The role of the universities in advancing citizenship and social justice in the 21st century. *Education, Citizenship and Social Justice* 5: 5–37.

Henkel, M. 1997. Academic values and the university as corporate enterprise. *Higher Education Quarterly* 51, no. 2: 134–43.

Lynch, K. 1995. Equality and resistance in higher education. *International Studies in Sociology of Education* 5, no. 1: 93–111.

Lynch, K. 1999. *Equality in education*. Chapter 9. Dublin: Gill and Macmillan.

Lynch, K., M. Crean, and M. Moran. 2009. Equality and social justice: The university as a site of struggle. In *The Routledge international handbook of sociology of education*, ed. M. Apple, S.J. Ball, and L.A. Gandin, 296–305. New York: Routledge.

Lynch, K. and C. O'Neill. 1994. The colonisation of social class in education. *British Journal of Sociology of Education* 15, no. 3: 307–24.

Marginson, S. 2006. Dynamics of global competition in higher education. *Higher Education* 52, no. 1: 1–39.

Martinelli, A. 2008. Sociology in political practice and public discourse. *Current Sociology* 56, no. 3: 361–70.

McDonnell, P. 2007. *Disability and society*. Dublin: Blackhall Press.

Nowotny, H., P. Scott, and M. Gibbons. 2001. *Re-thinking science*. Cambridge: Polity Press.

O'Connor, P. 2006. Private troubles, public issues: The Irish sociological imagination. *The Irish Journal of Sociology* 15, no. 2: 5–22.

Oliver, M. 1992. Changing the social relations of research production. *Disability, Handicap and Society* 7, no. 2: 101–14.

Reay, D. 2000. 'Dim dross': Marginalised women both inside and outside the academy. *Women's Studies International Forum* 23, no. 1: 13–21.

Rutherford, J. 2005. Cultural studies in the corporate university. *Cultural Studies* 19, no. 3: 297–317.

Sayer, A. 2006. Language and significance or the importance of import. *Journal of Language and Politics* 5, no. 3: 449–71.

Slaughter, S., and L.L. Leslie. 2001. Expanding and elaborating the concept of academic capitalism. *Organization* 8, no. 2: 154–61.

Slaughter, S., and G. Rhoades. 2004. *Academic capitalism in the new economy.* Baltimore, MD: John Hopkins University Press.

Steier, F.S. 2003. The changing nexus: Tertiary education institutions, the marketplace and the state. *Higher Education Quarterly* 57, no. 2: 158–80.

Thompson, J.B. 1990. *Ideology and modern culture.* Cambridge: Polity Press.

Tilly, C. 1998. *Durable inequality.* Berkeley: University of California Press.

Walker, S., and L. Barton, eds. 1983. *Gender, class and education.* Barcombe: The Falmer Press.

Webster, F. 2004. Cultural studies and sociology at and after the closure of the Birmingham School. *Cultural Studies* 18, no. 6: 847–62.

The heterodoxy of student voice: challenges to identity in the sociology of disability and education

Susan J. Peters

College of Education, Michigan State University, East Lansing, Michigan, USA

This article explores the contributions of students' voices in order to highlight some issues that have been central to disability studies – issues of identities, and their correlations to power, temporality, inclusivity, and place among the most salient to contemporary theories in the sociology of disability and education. Building on previous work that recognizes students' insights through the metaphors of street-wise philosophers, image-makers, and jazz improvisationists, I then chart a course for assessing theoretical frameworks in sociology and their applications to education, as well as to disability studies. Essentially, student voices offer opportunities for critical self-reflection as a disability studies scholar, as well as for reflection on the contributions of disability studies and sociology as a whole, leading to a transformative vision of the central tenets and tasks before us. The approach taken throughout this analysis is informed by Len Barton's call for a politics of hope.

Introduction: student voice

If you found out what they're not good at and put a label on them they would feel real low because you are messing around with their weakness. And no one wants you to play with their weakness because you can say too much about it. (Maenzanise, student-educator 1998[1])

An identity is never given, received or attained: only the interminable and indefinitely phantasmic process of identification endures. (Derrida 1998, 28)

Both this student and Derrida defy categorization of themselves. As a teacher, I have had the distinct privilege of listening to and learning from student-educators,[2] like the one quoted above, for several decades. In the face of institutional schooling's attempts at surveillance, control, and segregation, these students have, more often than not, defied categorizations, bypassed low expectations, and challenged injustices. In the process, they have taught me the meaning and value of life. Their defiance and rebellion also reveal reams about the conditions in schools, and their mistaken purposes. I believe that their voices also provide an interstice for re-examining some central tenets in the sociology of disability and education.

In this article, then, I will explore the contributions of students' voices in order to highlight an issue that has been central to disability studies – the issue of disability identity, and its correlation to power, temporality, inclusivity, and place among the most salient to contemporary theories in the sociology of disability and education. Interspersed with student-educator voices, the voices of teachers as learners (my own and others) provide a back-drop for critical introspection. This article highlights and builds on previous work (Peters, Klein, and Shadwick 1998) that recognizes students' insights through the metaphors of street-wise philosophers, image-makers, and jazz improvisation-ists. I then chart a course for assessing theoretical frameworks in sociology and disability studies with a particular focus on disability identity within the context of education in schools.

Essentially, student voices offer opportunities for critical self-reflection as a disability studies scholar, as well as for reflection on the contributions of disability studies and sociology as a whole, leading to a transformative vision of the central tenets and tasks before us. While the students' experiences I describe take place in secondary schools within the United States, their strug-gles to develop a positive identity resonate with the experiences conveyed to me by students I have come to know in other countries and contexts. The approach taken throughout this analysis is informed as well by Len Barton's call for a politics of hope: 'Hope is essential in the struggle for change. It involves a recognition of the unacceptable nature of the present conditions and relations, a desire to be in a different situation and a conviction that this is possible' (Barton 2001, 3).

Exploring identity: 'How does it feel to be a problem?'

> Between me and the other world there is ever an unasked question, 'How does it feel to be a problem?' (DuBois 1897)

> Everyone has problems and alter-eagles [sic][3] to maintain. And mine is to succeed in life and not let anyone else be pulling me down. (Mashingaidze, student-educator)

In a collaborative study of high school students identified as 'learning disabled' (LD),[4] I asked the question 'How does it feel to be a problem?' (Peters, Klein, and Shadwick 1998, 99). I first met these students in their senior-year special education Language Arts class. Their teacher had invited me to join the class and to work with them to improve their writing skills before they graduated. The urban high school in which this class met was composed almost entirely of African Americans. Most of the students in this class had been identified as LD early in their schooling. The label qualified them for special education services.

In this high school, as in countless high schools throughout the United States, these services are typically provided in segregated classrooms, constituting re-segregation by race and gender in otherwise integrated schools. Further, students of color are at extreme risk of being over-represented in special education. Black students in particular, in some states, are almost six times more likely to be labeled LD than a White student (Ferri and Connor 2006, 4). Darling-Hammond (2004, 21) reports that the graduation rate of 71% for African-American students in 2002 dropped to 59.5% in 2003. For African-American students in special education, the rate is thought to be lower than 50%. In 2004, new federal requirements for meeting proficiency levels on standardized tests resulted in a new operational definition for learning disabilities: students are labeled as LD if they have such low test scores that they seem unlikely to meet the established proficiency level by the time of the next test (White and Rosenbaum 2008, 104).

In asking the question 'How does it feel to be a problem?' I was concerned with the ways in which the students in this particular urban high school responded to the experience of social segregation and low academic expectations during the course of their schooling. As with the courses I teach at the university level, I approached teaching and learning in this Language Arts class from Paolo Freire's perspective of *education for critical consciousness* (Freire 1996). In our first session together, I shared with them the transcript of a speech I gave in the early 1990s to a group of parents of youth with disabilities. This speech introduced the concepts of the medical model of disability (an individual deficit as an innate characteristic) and the social model of disability (a socially constructed concept of difference in relation to the environment). The speech highlighted my own experiences as a disabled person since 1974:

> People with disabilities have been called many things. I have labeled the worst name calling the 'In Words': *in*valid, *in*competent, *in*spirational … I have a dream that someday people won't use a label when referring to me, but that they will call me by the name my parents gave me when I was born: Susan Jeanne Peters. I dream that I will be neither invalid nor inspirational. I want to be just an ordinary person who happens to use a wheelchair. I look forward to the day when it's ordinary to be different. The day that we recognize that our differences are what we all have in common. (Peters 1991, 194)

Students identified with my perspective, and it spurred a lively discussion. They shared with me the names that they had been called: 'retarded', 'backward', idiot. LD became an epithet for 'loco dummies' (crazy idiots) that was created and used by other students in their high school. They wondered out loud why they had been labeled in the first place, speculating that their identification as LD had been a combination of missing school, falling behind, and acting out in class by refusing to do work they considered boring and irrelevant. They felt an overwhelming sense of injustice toward the ways they had been treated – shunted off to separate classes and made to feel excluded. As one student-educator, Sekesai, put it:

> There are some people
> That just beat you any kind of way,
> No matter who you are
> Or what classes you are in.
> There are those who think that they're better than you
> And those who treat you special
> And those who think
> You can't do anything right.

These students' speculations:

> echo a small but growing body of evidence that views learning disability as the result of poor teaching and of a system increasingly unwilling to accept students who do not fit the expectations and structure of 'typical' students in the 'regular' classroom. (Peters, Klein, and Shadwick 1998, 106)

Their discussion in this initial session was both complex and intriguing. From this discussion, the students began to document their experiences in writing. They shared their writing with each other, gave feedback and asked questions, encouraging and assisting their classmates to delve more deeply into the meaning of their life experiences through a developing critical consciousness. Several themes in relation to their struggles to achieve a positive identity emerged from their responses to the 'problem' of disability in their lives. The following three sections characterize the ways in which they responded to these struggles.

Forging identity as image-makers

> In my class there are some students who want to learn and some who don't want to learn so what we did was those of us who want to learn sit on one side of the room and those of us who don't want to learn sit on the other side. (Mugwindiri, student-educator)

> In 1987, on receiving my first teaching schedule within a New York City high school, I was told that all my classes would comprise students with learning disabilities. It was the first time I had heard the label. It struck me as odd then and it strikes me as odd now. In those days, I assumed the word 'disability' was synonymous with 'inability' and naively thought, 'How strange! There must be people who cannot learn, and it is now my job to teach them.' (Teacher-learner; Connor 2008, 7)

Students in today's schools have to juggle a multitude of schedules, academic expectations, and social relationships. Forging an identity amidst this entangled web of experiences requires a constant juggling act. Students perceived as LD have an invisible disability; they do not look different from others. As a consequence, their disability only becomes evident when their labels are discovered by others. One student, Mandivamba, asked:

> Let's say what if they found out (I was in special ed)? Would they still be my friends? Would they still go to the park with me? Or would they just blow my cover and tell everyone I was in special ed?

This student, and many of his peers, developed complicated strategies to hide their status markers. Their special education teacher became an accomplice in managing their secret. She covered the window in her classroom and excused students from class before the scheduled time so that her students would not be seen leaving the 'special ed room', which was evident due to its location in the school and its small class size.

Individually, students resisted their images as 'loco dummies' in a number of ways. One strategy the students chose was to seat themselves on opposite sides of the classroom, as in the student-educator quoted in the introduction to this section. Choosing sides reveals an individual agency that resists negative images. In essence, students have learned to manipulate the system. Crossing borders becomes a process of developing new ways of thinking about themselves and others. The students also play with images by turning the tables and 'messing around' with the notion of other people's weakness. They demonstrate resilience by consciously redefining the concept of LD through manipulation of the rules of the game, transforming negative images into positive ones.

A few teachers, such as David Connor, also struggle with the image of inability to learn that the term 'learning disability' implies. As David began his teaching career in New York City schools, he relates that he became distrustful of this image and the system of identification and segregated classes that supported it. As with my own experience in urban schools, David came to the realization that 'disability is political' (Connor 2008, 16). Throughout my own professional career and life experiences as a disabled person, I have also struggled with low expectations inherent in the politics of disability. I have resisted others image of me as a perpetual student, rather than as a professional in my own right.

Becoming street-wise philosophers

> Ain't nobody perfect. Never give up and you'll make it. (Mashingaidze, student-educator)

> One of the basic questions I have asked myself repeatedly is 'How can we weave our disabilities (if they are disabilities) into the fabric of our lives, rather than

reducing them to isolated traits or innate deficiencies?' (Teacher-learner; Peters 1996, 225)

In the United States, slightly more than 50% of students identified as 'learning disabled' drop out of school before graduation (Darling-Hammond 2004). I recognized that the students in this urban high school were an elite group: they were still in school. To accomplish this task, they had demonstrated resilience in the face of a multitude of institutional and attitudinal barriers. The practical philosophies expressed through their narratives provided windows to understand this resilience. For example, the student quoted in the introduction to this section, who recognized that nobody's perfect, entitled her essay 'Can't Miss Reality.' In this essay, she expressed the belief that she would succeed in life because she used her experiences to learn how to deal with others and to handle difficult situations.

Another student, Unhu, echoed this belief: 'Labeling makes you one of two things – weak or strong.' Being called names like 'loco dummy' was something she faced every day, but she expressed the belief that it made her strong and able to 'withstand a lot of stuff from people.'

Behind these voices – the bits and pieces of their thinking that they chose to share and to which I have applied my own interpretations for better or worse – lie life experiences woven with violence, uncertainty, and risks. Yet, when asked about their future dreams and aspirations, their responses belie stereotypes deriving from a plethora of statistics on low socioeconomic status of minority youth. Most of the students expressed plans to attend college. To attain this goal, they asserted their need to work hard, have determination, motivation, patience, responsibility, and self-confidence. For example, one student, Mashingaidze stated confidently: 'I'm going to succeed in a lot of things like graduating, going to college, and getting a good job that will support me and mines.'

Expressing a desire for jazz improvisation

Some teachers have that learning class … We want to learn too. (Hazvizikanwi, student-educator)

Besides working on different things per class hour, each student is on a different level of interest and ability. What a challenge! (Teacher-learner; Peters, Klein, and Shadwick 1998, 110)

For many students in this urban high school, learning seems like a dirge or a march: repetitious and slow. One student, Hazvizikanwi, observed: 'Some teachers have us learning out of the same book year after year, then we never have the time to learn that much out of a regular book.' Singled out for special education classes, students feel out of step with their peers in 'regular' class. Learning feels discordant: 'Say [for example] if we both had the same book and they [regular students] would be on page 167 and we would be on page 66 ...'

These students want a faster tempo and opportunities to improvise. They break the monotony of textbook instruction by moonwalking to Michael Jackson's music during class. They carry on side commentaries during their lessons that seem to ebb and flow like musical crescendos. Taken together, their words and actions ask for a script that encourages solos, yet with opportunities for harmony as well.

As a result of listening to students, for me the question became not 'How does it feel to be a problem?', but 'How does it feel to recognize that school is the problem?' and 'Am I a part of the problem?'

Retrospection: from Erving Goffman's disability as abomination of the body to Garland-Thomson's visual activists

Disability studies as a discipline emanated from grass-roots organizations and their persistent quest for a change in identity of, by, and for disabled people. The social model of disability – promoted by organizations such as the Union of the Physically Impaired in Britain, and the Centers for Independent Living in the United States –insisted on a paradigm shift. This shift viewed disability not from the traditional perspective as individual characteristic, but as a socially constructed experience of oppression imposed by physical, economic, educational, and political barriers to equal participation in society. Disability studies scholars took up this challenge by interrogating constructions of disability. While Disability studies scholars have utilized multiple disciplines to interrogate these constructions, theoretical frameworks from sociology have maintained a critical influence in much of the literature (Gabel and Peters 2004).[5]

Sociological frameworks seem particularly suited to challenging disability identity. 'Sociologists are always asking questions, sharpening the focus of concern and providing critiques of existing forms of social conditions and relations' (Barton 1996, 3). In respect to identity and its social construction, Disability Studies has been a critical friend to sociology. One of disability studies scholars' favorite foils is the sociologist, Erving Goffman (1963). Two examples of influential scholarship over the past 15 years come to mind. First, while acknowledging that Goffman's theory of stigma represented a significant advance over purely psychological conceptions of disability, Nancy Eiesland argues that his theory of stigma 'freezes the isolated stigmatized person in perpetual introductions and initial conversations' (Eiesland 1994, 61). By contrast, Eiesland utilizes a social minority-group model to develop an image of disabled people as embodying 'resourcefulness, independence, and persistence' (1994, 64). Second, Rosemarie Garland-Thomson, in her critically acclaimed book *Staring: How We Look*, uses Goffman's hierarchy of stigma designations between 'normals' and the 'stigmatized' as an analytical tool to develop the notion of stigmatized individuals as active agents or 'intentional meaning makers' by the ways that they 'realign the power inherent in staring by merging body and word in an act of self-making' (Garland-Thomson 2009, 139). She calls this process visual activism.

In the same vein, this shift from Goffman's disabled person as an object of stigma, to active subject has been central to my own work. In *The Politics of Disability Identity*, I argued that 'despite predominant symbols and rituals which carry negative conceptions of disability, some people with ascribed disabilities choose to embrace their difference as a positive identity marker ... This identity is often developed in spite of formidable barriers ...' (Peters 1996, 231). Much of my subsequent work has focused on understanding how positive identity develops and the ways in which it can be supported and sustained.

I am not alone in this work. In *Disability Politics*, Campbell and Oliver (1996) were among the first disability studies scholars to recognize and use disability voice prominently to demonstrate that collective agency in disability movements rests on the positive identities forged through awareness of disability as social oppression.

In the past decade, several other scholars have highlighted student voice, and the voices of disabled people. Nicholas Watson (2002) interviewed people with physical impairments regarding their ideas about health and health status. A significant theme that emerged demonstrated the importance of identity inherent in agency and resistance. Davis and Watson (2002) analyzed the dialogues of disabled children and discovered forms of resistance that countered stereotypes of disabled youth as passive, vulnerable and dependent. Most recently, in *Urban Narratives*, Connor (2008) focuses on the lives of working-class, minority students labeled as LD in urban schools. Their narratives contrast significantly from the professional literature. Connor offers examples of these students' empowerment that counter notions that they are merely passive victims of social forces.

In *Exploring Disability*, Barnes, Mercer, and Shakespeare (1999, 13) highlight a key feature of sociological approaches to the study of disability exemplified by the scholars cited above – the sociological imagination. This imagination critiques forms of society – school organization, structure and culture prominent among these forms. Barnes, Mercer, and Shakespeare (1999), drawing from Giddens (1982a, 26), argue that sociological imagination also prompts an awareness of 'alternative futures'. In this endeavor to imagine alternative futures, 'sociology cannot be a neutral intellectual endeavor, indifferent to the practical consequences of its analysis ...' (Giddens 1982b, vii). Educators and disability studies scholars, are especially drawn to using sociological imagination as a tool for examining the construction of disability in schools.

Looking forward: transformation and hope

In class discussions, informal conversations, self-expression in journal writing and poetry, the students in the high school that I was privileged to learn from defied categorizations and challenged injustices. Their voices provide a powerful heterodoxy, or counterpoint, to the root paradigm of disability as innate individual deficiency inherent in special education policies and practices. Specifically, heterodoxy of student voice provides two key notions for re-examining disability identity from sociological imagination: resistance and resilience. These notions also stand in opposition to traditional views of disability as stigma and social construction, creating an interstice for change.

Resistance: teaching to transgress

First, heterodoxy of voice provides a powerful sociological imagination for resisting the stigma of exclusion and deficit thinking. The student-educator voices highlighted in this article have subjected disability to a social analysis through their street-wise philosophies that pushes back, turning the tables by 'messing around' with weaknesses. Julie Allan, in her work on rethinking inclusive education, argues that this resistance constitutes the critical challenge of both teachers and students in schools:

> If the participants in the inclusion struggle were able to do so as practical philosophers, experimenting with and experiencing inclusion, difference could possibly become a source of interest and intrigue –a puzzle—rather than a problem to be defined and managed. (Allan 2008, 102)

The process of critical consciousness employed by the students in the Language Arts class demonstrated experimentation through reciprocity between reflection and action. Naming injustices in their schooling experiences, their resistance took the form of action. They sought remedies and formulated a manifesto with several practical recommendations for changes in their school practices and policies. These recommendations were circulated widely among the staff and students, and acted as a catalyst for change. For example, the school administrators gave students more of a collective voice through establishing a student council to advise and guide decisions. Senior dance plans and football game attendance policies were made in collaboration with the student council, rather than handed down as edicts from the central office. Lock-downs during lunch-time were no longer enforced. Student-leaders stationed at entrances to the school welcomed visitors and directed them to classrooms.

These students' special education teacher supported proactive resistance. Acting as a referee, trainer and coach, she encouraged her students by emphasizing and reinforcing their talents for improvisation – both in school and out of school. Her teaching exemplified a form of 'engaged pedagogy', or creative engagement with students' lives. Bell hooks describes engaged pedagogy as 'the mutual interplay of thinking, writing and sharing ideas' (1994, 205). She concludes:

> the classroom, with all its limitations, remains a location of possibility. In that field of possibility we have the opportunity to labor for freedom, to demand of

ourselves and our comrades, an openness of mind and heart that allows us to face reality even as we collectively imagine ways to move beyond boundaries, to transgress. (hooks 1994, 207)

Similarly, Julie Allan describes a school in which the head teacher implemented a children's rights framework, forming a small group of children to analyze inclusion practices in their school. The group called themselves SNOG: Special Needs Observation Group. Allan reports that this group 'excelled in identifying the barriers to participation and encouraging the whole school community to think and act more inclusively' (2008, 107).

Resilience: problematising place, knowledge and power relations

The second form of sociological imagination – resilience – directly problematises the unequal distribution of knowledge and power. Student voices fly in the face of the despair engendered by a critical body of literature on social oppression and stigma. Their voices provide a heterodoxy characterized by resilience. Uncovering oppression at the societal level has been a necessary prerequisite for challenging and changing the ways schools perpetuate injustices. Yet, analysis at the individual level through student voices provides hope for transformation.

Resilience demands attention, not only to removing barriers such as the policies and practices that require students to juggle their images, but to empowering and enabling student agency. The students in the language arts class were the elite who had demonstrated their resilience – struggling against barriers, and remaining in school. How many more students would remain in school if resilience was actively taught and engaged? As the student who wrote 'Can't Miss Reality' observed:

> Special education has really taught me a lot, like how to express yourself, deal with others, and how to handle other situations. I like special attention. That's what most people, especially ones with emotional problems need – special attention. I know most regular students want that but can't get it. (Mashingaidze, student-educator)

Must the mechanism for resilience and positive identity emanate from identification and placement in segregated special education classrooms? Individual agency, expressed through particular forms of both resilience and resistance, challenge a stigmatizing societal identity and provide an interstice for developing a sociological imagination that recognizes the 'interrelationship between history, biography, context and structural factors' (Barton 2001, 8). The central role of identity within this interrelationship is not given, received or attained, but an enduring process underscored by desire and the conviction that success is possible. Students recognize this wisdom, but will those who teach them, who theorize about them, and who are responsible for the conditions in their schools recognize it as well? Therein lie the possibilities for transformation and hope.

Notes

1. The source for the student-educator quotes in this article is their written work developed during the special education Language Arts class in which the author participated. All names are pseudonyms they chose for themselves from the Shona language of Zimbabwe. An anthology of their work was compiled and distributed (with their permission) in a monograph that the students entitled 'From our Voice.' Copies may be obtained from the author.
2. Throughout this article, I use the terms 'student-educator' and 'teacher-learner' to emphasize the notion that students may be teachers, and teachers may be learners. This notion recognizes the reciprocal relations between teaching and learning.
3. This student was using a hand-held electronic spell-check computer device that suggested alternatives to misspelled words. The student was actually looking for the word 'alter-ego.' The misuse of the word 'alter-ego' is actually more expressive in the context of the meaning the student was attempting to convey. In recognition of the power that this term conveys as a metaphor, we used it in the title of our original article 'From Our Voices: Special Education and the "Alter-eagle" Problem' (Peters, Klein, and Shadwick 1998).
4. In the United States, learning disability is defined by the federal government as 'a disorder in one or more of the basic psychological processes involved in understanding or in using language, spoken or written, which disorder may manifest itself in imperfect ability to listen, think, speak, read, write, spell, or do mathematical calculations. Such term does not include a learning problem that is primarily the result of visual, hearing, or motor disabilities, of mental retardation, of emotional disturbance, or of environmental, cultural, or economic disadvantage' (Individuals Disabilities Education Act 2004: 20 U.S.C. §1401 [30]).
5. The reader is encouraged to refer to Gabel and Peters (2004) for a comprehensive review of a significant number of disability scholars' contributions to theoretical frameworks from sociology.

References

Allan, J. 2008. *Rethinking inclusive education: The philosophers of difference in practice.* Dordrecht, The Netherlands: Springer.

Barnes, C., G. Mercer, and T. Shakespeare. 1999. *Exploring disability: A sociological introduction.* Malden, MA: Blackwell Publishing.

Barton, L. 1996. Sociology and disability: Some emerging issues. In *Disability & society: Emerging issues and insights,* ed. L. Barton, 3–17. London: Longman.

Barton, L. 2001. Disability, struggle and the politics of hope. In *Disability, politics and the struggle for change,* ed. L. Barton, 1–10. London: David Fulton.

Campbell, J., and M. Oliver. 1996. *Disability politics: Understanding our past, changing our future.* London: Routledge.

Connor, D.J. 2008. *Urban narratives: Portraits in progress.* New York: Peter Lang.

Darling-Hammond, L. 2004. From 'Separate but Equal' to 'No Child Left Behind': The collision of new standards and old inequalities. In *Many children left behind,* ed. D. Meier and G. Wood, 3–32. Boston: Beacon Press.

Davis, J., and N. Watson. 2002. Countering stereotypes of disability: Disabled children and resistance. In *Disability/postmodernity: Embodying disability theory,* ed. M. Corker and T. Shakespeare, 159–74. London: Continuum.

Derrida, J. 1998. *Monolingualism of the other: Or, the prosthesis of origin.* Stanford, CA: Stanford University Press.

DuBois, W.E.B. 1897. Strivings of the negro people. *Atlantic Monthly* 80: 194–8.

Eiesland, N.L. 1994. *The disabled god: Toward a liberatory theology of disability.* Nashville, TN: Abingdon Press.

Freire, P. 1996. *Education for critical consciousness.* New York: Continuum.

Gabel, S., and S. Peters. 2004. Presage of a paradigm shift? Beyond the social model of disability toward resistance theories of disability. *Disability & Society* 19, no. 6: 585–600.

Garland-Thomson, R. 2009. *Staring: How we look.* Oxford: Oxford University Press.

Giddens, A. 1982a. *Sociology: A brief but critical introduction.* London: Macmillan.

Giddens, A. 1982b. *Profiles and critiques in social theory.* London: Macmillan.

Goffman, E. 1963. *Stigma: Notes on the management of spoiled identity.* Englewood Cliffs, NJ: Prentice-Hall.

Ferri, B., and D.J. Connor. 2006. *Reading resistance: Discourses of exclusion in desegregation and inclusion debates.* New York: Peter Lang.

hooks, bell. 1994. *Teaching to transgress: Education as the practice of freedom.* New York: Routledge.

Peters, S.J. 1991. Changing images for people with disabilities. *Coalition Quarterly,* 8, nos 1&2: 6–11.

Peters, S. 1996. The politics of disability identity. In *Disability and society: Emerging issues and insights,* ed. L. Barton, 215–34. London: Longman.

Peters, S.J., A. Klein, and C. Shadwick. 1998. From our voices: Special education and the 'alter-eagle' problem. In *When children don't learn: Student failure and the culture of teaching,* ed. B.M. Franklin, 99–115. New York: Teachers College Press.

Watson, N. 2002. Enabling identity: Disability, self and citizenship. In *The disability reader: Social science perspectives,* ed. T. Shakespeare, 147–62. London: Continuum.

White, K., and J. Rosenbaum. 2008. Inside the black box of accountability: How high-stakes accountability alters school culture and the classification and treatment of students and teachers. In *No Child Left Behind and the reduction of the achievement gap,* ed. A. Sadovnik et al., 97–116. New York: Routledge.

The sociology of disability and the struggle for inclusive education

Julie Allan

University of Stirling, Institute of Education, Stirling, UK

This article charts the emergence of the sociology of disability and examines the areas of contestation. These have involved a series of erasures and absences – the removal of the body from debates on the social model of disability; the disappearance of the Other from educational policies and practices; and the absence of academics from political discourses and action. The paper considers the contribution of the sociology of disability to inclusive education and examines some of the objections currently being voiced. It ends with some reflections on the possibilities for academics within the sociology of disability to pursue alternative forms of engagement and outlines a series of duties that they might undertake.

Introduction

The sociology of disability, the foundations of which were established by a small number of key scholars (Len Barton, Sally Tomlinson and Mike Oliver), is marked by a significant shift in the analysis of the nature and causes of disability from individualistic to social and material frames of reference. This field, however, has been a somewhat troubled and contested one, with intensive battles over identity and presence and a series of active erasures and absences – the removal of the body from the social model of disability; the disappearance of the Other from educational policies and practices; and disability academics' own absence from political discourse and action. These battles and erasures have done little to advance the struggle for inclusive education, and more voices than ever before can be heard challenging the very idea. This article charts the emergence of the sociology of disability and examines the areas of contestation. It considers the contribution of the sociology of disability to inclusive education and examines some of the objections to it currently being voiced. The paper ends with some reflections on the possibilities for alternative forms of engagement by academics within the sociology of disability and outlines a series of duties that may make inclusive education more feasible and more capable of making a material difference to the lives of disabled children.

The sociology of disability

The sociology of disability emerged in the 1980s as a direct challenge to the weighty paradigm of special education, with its fixation on individual deficits and remedies. Len Barton's (1988) *The Politics of Special Educational Needs*, Sally Tomlinson's (1981) *Educational Subnormality: A Study in Decision-making* and (1982) *A Sociology of Special Education*, Len Barton and Sally Tomlinson's (1984) jointly edited *Special Education and Social Interests*, and Julienne Mongon, Denis Ford and Maurice Whelan's (1982) *Special Education and Social Control: Invisible Disasters* abruptly turned the gaze away from the child and highlighted the role of institutional structures and practices in producing school failure. Disabled academics Mike Oliver (1996, 1999), Colin Barnes (Barnes and Mercer 2002), Sally French (1993, 1994; Swain and French 2008), Tom Shakespeare (2006; Barnes, Mercer, and Shakespeare 1999), Jenny Morris (1991) and Carol Thomas (1999, 2007) have also provided significant sociological analyses that have identified disability as being produced by environmental, structural and attitudinal barriers.

  Barton has subsequently outlined the clear function and duty of the sociology of disability:

> A political analysis which is inspired by a desire for transformative change and that constitutes hope at the centre of the struggles … At both an individual and collective level a crucial task is to develop a theory of political action which also involves the generation of tactics or strategies for its implementation. This is a difficult but essential agenda. (2001, 3)

This agenda has been difficult for sociology in general as well as for the sociology of disability, and there has been much agonising about the challenge of insulating research from value bias whilst contributing to social change through research (Gewirtz and Cribb 2006). Hammersley (2008) has argued forcefully that politically committed research is incompatible with academic rigour, but Gewirtz and Cribb (2008) and others (Flvyberg 2001; Walford, Halpin, and Troyna 1994) have insisted that a sociology bound by ethical reflexivity can be both more responsible and methodologically rigorous. For the sociology of disability, there seems to have been no problem in accepting the political commitment but some difficulties in enacting it.

Erasures in the field

The sociology of disability, as a field, has struggled to maintain both a presence and an authority. It is possible to discern three significant erasures within the field of sociology of disability that have had negative consequences for it. The first of these concerns the efforts to remove the disabled body from the social model of disability. The second is the more widespread disappearance of the Other, disabled or different in some other way, from within educational policies and practices; and the third is the absence of academics (partly by their own hand) from political discourse and action.

Missing persons in the social model of disability

Mike Oliver has expressed his disappointment that the social model of disability, developed by disabled people, has not been used as a tool for altering the material circumstances of disabled people and fostering inclusion and wishes that people would use the social model, rather than continue to debate it:

> I wish people would stop talking about it. The social model is not some kind of conceptual device to debate. The social model is a tool that we should use to try and produce changes in the world, changes in what we do. What I hoped from that was that people would start using it and what we would actually see was not 'what are the theoretical underpinnings of the social model?' ... but 'this is what I actually did with the social model. This is how I took it into a particular school or a particular social work agency. This is what we did with it and this is whether it worked or not'. (Allan and Slee 2008, 88)

The social model was developed to counter the formidable tragedy discourse that surrounds disabled people and that depicts disability as a deficit, a tragedy and *'abnormal,* and something to be avoided at all costs' (Oliver and Barnes 1996, 66; original emphasis). However, as Swain and French (2008) point out, the tragedy model of disability plays on people's fears of their own mortality and vulnerability and is ingrained in society, with the effect of silencing and excluding disabled people.

Shakespeare (2006) contends that there are significant problems with the social model and it has become an obstacle to the development of the disability movement and to disability studies:

> I have come to the conclusion that the British social model of disability studies has reached a dead end, having taken a wrong turn back in the 1970s when the Union of Physically Impaired Against Segregation (UPIAS) social model conception became the dominant UK understanding of disability ... At one time I was a critical friend of the social model, defending it against external attack (Shakespeare and Watson 1997): I am now among those who argue that it should be abandoned. (Shakespeare 2006, 3–5)

The inability to come up with an adequate theory of disability is, according to Paterson and Hughes (2000, 42), 'one of the more spectacular failures of modern sociological research'. Shakespeare suggests that the problems of the social model are, paradoxically, also its successes. It was developed as a political intervention rather than a social theory; it was strongly tied into identity politics; and it was defended as *correct* by its initial proponents, but not subjected to revision over the 30 years of its life. Separating impairment from disability was an important move to privilege the material causes of disability and to force the removal of these, but it has led to a disavowal of impairment – because 'frailty offends' (Hughes 2009, 401) – which many disabled people have found difficult to accept:

> As individuals, most of us simply cannot pretend with any conviction that our impairments are irrelevant because they influence every aspect of our lives. We must find a way to integrate them into our whole experience and to identify for the sake of our physical and emotional well-being and, subsequently, for our capacity to work against Disability. (Crow 1992, 7)

French is sympathetic to the need to present disability in a 'straightforward, uncomplicated manner in order to convince a very sceptical world' (1993, 24) that it is society, rather than individuals, that has to be changed. Nevertheless, the dogmatic defence of the social model as orthodoxy is, according to Shakespeare, problematic and has contributed to the exclusion of the disability movement:

> Alone amongst radical movements, the UK disability rights tradition has, like a fundamentalist religion, retained its allegiance to a narrow reading of its founding assumptions. (Shakespeare 2006, 34)

Shakespeare and other commentators (e.g. Paterson and Hughes 1999) have contended that the social model needs to become more sophisticated if it is to be relevant to the lives of disabled people or at least used more reflexively (Corker 1999). This heightened sophistication can be seen in two separate refinements of the social model. The first is the development of an 'affirmation model', led by John Swain and Sally French (2008), which rejects tragic depictions of disabled people and associated notions of dependency and abnormality and affirms and validates their experiences. It also acknowledges the significance of individuals' impairments, something that was not possible within the social model. The second refinement entails enabling disabled people to reclaim their disabled bodies from the purely social construction of disability (Shakespeare 2006; Hughes 2009) and procuring vulnerability and frailty as 'an inalienable condition of becoming' (Shildrick 2002, 85). This, argues Hughes (2009), allows the binaries of disability/impairment and the disabled/normal body to be dismantled or at least undermined. Both of these developments of the social model have the potential to re-politicise disability and to provide a new subjectification of the disabled person who is simultaneously impaired and oppressed (Shakespeare 2006).

The disappeared Other in education

Education is characterised by what Derrida (1990, 1993) calls aporias, which are oppositional or contradictory imperatives. Such oppositions – for example, between raising achievement and promoting inclusion, or between educating individuals to be able hold their own in the competitive world, and ensuring those individuals can collaborate, cooperate and understand their civic responsibilities – are constructed in educational policies and practices as *choices* to be made. They are often resolved by privileging one imperative over another, in a way that the obligation to the 'Other' – the disabled person or the individual with learning difficulties – is denied. This forgetfulness of the Other becomes formalised and justified through policies and practices that endorse solution, resolution and 'the desire for translation, agreement and univocity' (Derrida 1992, 78). The decisiveness called for within education forces closure and is, according to Derrida (1992, 26), irresponsible and a 'madness', because the way forward is clear and possible alternatives are removed. All that remains is a technical solution: 'one simply applies or implements a program' (Derrida 1992, 41). It produces injustice:

> Injustice – not to mention racism, nationalism and imperialism – begins when one loses sight of the transcendence of the Other and forgets that the State, with its institutions, is informed by the proximity of my relation to the Other. (Critchley 1999, 233)

In education, frameworks of accountability and performativity are defended by governments on the basis of inclusion, entitlement and equity, when evidence points to the injustices produced by such frameworks for both professionals and those for whom they are responsible (Allan 2008; Booth 2003; Smyth 2000; Torrance 2008). In the United Kingdom, injustices in relation to disability, ethnicity, class and gender are abundantly clear (Gillborn 2008; Gamarnikow and Green 2009). Paradoxically the removal of the Other comes through a pathologising and naming of individuals in relation (only) to their deficits. Thomas calls this a 'closure on learning' (2008, 7), which produces and reinforces disabled, ethnic, class and gendered identities as both failures and in their 'sameness' (Garrison 2008, 273) to others.

Absent colleagues

Barton and Clough (1995) have underlined the obligations and responsibilities of those working in the field of disability, especially within academic positions, and have posed these as questions:

- What responsibilities arise from the privileges I have as a result of my social position?
- How can I use my knowledge and skills to challenge, for example, the forms of oppression disabled people experience?
- Does my writing and speaking reproduce a system of domination or challenge that system? (Barton and Clough 1995, 144)

Academics have, however, been slow to take up these responsibilities and, as Davis (2002, 10) notes, political and academic movement around disability 'has been at best, a first or second wave enterprise'. Skrtic (1995, 80) sees the problem as lying with inclusive education researchers simply following the same patterns as in the integration debate and engaging in 'naïve pragmatism', merely criticising special education practices and not engaging in systematic analysis of their underlying assumptions. Erevelles (2006, 363) recalls how, as a doctoral student, her efforts to initiate political discussions about the inter-connections between race and disability were met with 'polite disinterest' by her teachers and led to 'non-conversations'. Oliver (1999) has been more vociferous in his criticism of academics' failure to use their positions and power to alter the material conditions of disabled people. He has described them as 'parasitic upon disabled people' (Oliver 1999, 184) and has accused those undertaking research of having appropriated the experiences of disabled people and, in so doing, of '*shitting* disabled people' (1999, 187; original emphasis). The enjoinder to non-disabled academics is not to withdraw from disability research but to 'put disabled people at the centre of the picture' (Shakespeare 2006, 186) and to be accountable to organisations of disabled people.

Several academics have argued that the 'audit culture' (Strathern 1997, 2000) within higher education has undermined academic culture and autonomy (Paterson 2003) and limited their capacity to influence communities and their values. Evans (2004, 63) contends that the regulatory practices within univer-sities is 'producing fear and little else' and is 'killing thinking', while Furedi (2004, vii) wonders 'where have all the intellectuals gone?' A further danger for the intellectual, according to Said (1994), comes from the limitations and constraints of professionalism that encourage conformity rather than critique:

> By professionalism I mean thinking of your work as an intellectual as some-thing you do for a living, between the hours of nine and five with one eye on the clock, and another cocked at what is considered to be proper, profes-sional behaviour – not rocking the boat, not straying outside the accepted paradigms or limits, making yourself marketable and above all presentable, hence uncontroversial and unpolitical and *objective* (Said 1994, 55; empha-sis in original)

Derrida reminds us that to profess, either as members of a professional group or as academics, is to make a performative declaration of faith and commit-ment that exceeds techno-scientific knowledge (Cohen 2001) even though it may be reducible to this. Said's point that the commitment to professionalism, and the accountability that goes with it, can produce a kind of quietism is well made. I would suggest, however, that frameworks of accountability, far from overwhelming and constraining academics, enable them to evade responsibil-ity for the Other.

Struggling to include?

The sociology of disability has successfully directed attention to the structural and material causes of disability and failure and has oriented analyses of inclusive education towards the identification of exclusionary pressures. The simultaneous analysis of exclusion and inclusion has been recognised by many scholars as vital if inclusive education is to be properly understood and enacted (Ballard 2003; Booth and Ainscow 1998). Yet, in spite of this awareness, we appear to be no closer to an understanding of how to achieve inclusive education. Dyson, Howes, and Roberts (2002), who undertook a systematic review of research on inclusion, found that few 'golden solutions' had been produced. At the same time, there is no shortage of *technical help* in the form of easy guides to inclusive education. These texts present as 'authoritative purveyors of technical knowledge' (Brantlinger 2006, 67) and portray idealised versions of classroom life and of children benefiting from interventions. They offer simple, easy to implement, strategies for managing difference, such as '60 research-based teaching strategies that help special learners succeed' (McNary 2005) or 'commonsense methods for children with special educational needs' (Westwood 2002), and fail to explore issues of inclusion, equity and justice in anything other than a superficial way. When beginning teachers encounter difference in their classrooms it bears no resemblance to the textbook portrayals. Although the problematic nature of these appears to be uniform, Brantlinger (2006, 45) takes particular exception to the US hardbacks – 'the big glossies'. Furthermore, the textbooks affect a sound theoretical base, but as Thomas (2008, 1) observes, they amount to little more than 'theory junk sculpture', a 'cacophany of incompatible explanations', in which 'plausible homily, mixed with large portions of psychoanalytic and psychological vocabulary, take the place of a rational consideration of children's behaviour at school'. A rational consideration might involve putting the social model to use, as Oliver (1996) recommended, and identifying and removing barriers to participation, but this is not forthcoming from the textbooks, which are instead intent on highlighting, and then generalising about, children's deficits. The textbooks command an authority that is reassuring, especially to new teachers, but their intent to persuade new teachers that difference is easily managed makes them deeply irresponsible.

Barton (1997) specified clearly that inclusive education involved the twofold activity of increasing participation and removing exclusionary barriers. Suspicions have been voiced, however, that inclusive education has merely been a new name under which exclusionary special education practices have been replicated (Slee 1993, 2001; Slee and Allan 2001). Slee (2003) has drawn attention to the oxymoronic nature of the term inclusive education itself, pointing out that schools were never meant to be for everyone and must, in order to function, position some individuals as failures, and indeed inclusion within classrooms may be an impossibility as long as the more widespread and systemic exclusion within the education system remains.

Researchers have reported serious resistance to inclusion by teachers (Croll and Moses 2000; Thomas and Vaughan 2004) and a lack of confidence in their capacity to deliver inclusion with existing resources (Hanko 2005). Macbeath et al. (2006) found teachers were positive about inclusion but did not see it as appropriate for children with complex emotional needs. Tom Shakespeare (2005) has suggested that there is a measure of 'hysteria', 'moral panic' and an 'alarming backlash against the principle of inclusion', while Dyson (2001, 27) contends that tensions within the inclusion movement have led to a 'recalibration' of inclusion which amounts to pleas for 'old fashioned integration'.

Even the 'architect' of inclusion, Mary Warnock, has subsequently claimed to regard the idea of inclusion to have been 'disastrous' (Warnock 2005, 22). In a pamphlet published by the Philosophy of Education Society of Great Britain, she declared it to have been a mistake to have thought that all children could succeed in mainstream schools and lamented that 'children are the casualities' (Warnock 2005, 14) of this mistake. Her call for a return to segregated schooling, at least for some people, was denounced roundly by inclusion commentators such as Barton (2005) and Norwich (2006), who expressed disappointment and puzzlement at her lack of familiarity with the field of inclusion and its current debates, but was seen as a vindication by others (Spurgeon 2006; Wing 2006) and as an indication that 'the tide is turning on SEN provision' (Gloucestershire Special Schools Protection League 2005). Although Barton (2005) elegantly dismissed Warnock's pronouncements as ignorant and offensive, he also expressed some concern about her 'naïve and politically reactionary demand' (Barton 2005, 4) for acceptance that 'even if inclusion is an ideal for society in general, it may not always be an ideal for school' (Warnock 2005, 43). He warned that such thinking, if realised in practice, 'will contribute to the building up of serious individual and socially divisive problems for the future' (Barton 2005, 4).

New forms of engagement

Try again. Fail Again. Fail better. (Beckett 1992: 101)

The troubles within the field of the sociology of disability have, I argue, limited its capacity as a transformative and political social theory and restricted the acquisition of knowledge about the means of accomplishing inclusive education. Whilst this is, in some respects, disappointing, it is the very disappointment that comes from the recognition of injustice that could provoke the need for a response from the sociology of disability that is ethical and that rescues disabled people, and the Other more generally, from obscurity and denial. Thus the failures caused by a lack of responsibility could be redressed by the establishment of an ethics that 'might be able to face and face down the iniquities of the present' (Critchley 2007, 88). Such an ethics, informed by Levinas (1969, 1999) and constituting a reorientation to human subjectivity, has as its core an absolute responsibility to the Other and an asymmetrical relation to the Other because of an inadequacy in the face of the demand of the Other (Critchley 2007). This relationship is both aporetic, in the sense of having double contradictory imperatives, and infinite:

> The idea of the infinite consists precisely and paradoxically in thinking more than what is thought while nevertheless conserving it in its excessive relation to thought. The idea of the infinite consists in grasping the ungraspable while nevertheless guaranteeing its status as ungraspable. (Levinas 1969, 19)

The relationship is also experienced as not benign, but as a responsibility that 'persecutes me with its sheer weight' (Critchley 2007, 59) and produces an absolute imperative towards the Other that is a 'gratuitous and non-transferable responsibility, as if they were chosen and unique – and in which the other were absolutely other, i.e … still incomparable and thus unique' (Levinas 1999, 170). This responsibility is inescapable:

> to be a 'self' is to be responsible before having done anything … I am not merely the origin of myself, but I am disturbed by the Other. Not judged by the Other, but condemned without being able to speak, persecuted. (Levinas 1996, 94)

It is also a vital part of what it is to be human: 'Let's face it. We're undone by each other. And if not, we're missing something' (Butler 2004, 43).

Academic 'duties'

Bourdieu maintains that it is vital that academics are protected from urgent duties and that they can be allowed to 'play seriously' (1998, 128):

> *Homo scholasticus* or *homo academicus* is someone who can play seriously because his or her state (or State) assures her the means to do so, that is, free time, outside the urgency of a practical situation. (Bourdieu 1998, 128)

An ethics could enable academics to have greater control and to engage in serious play. The foregrounding of the responsibility to the Other makes the academic's role explicitly a political one, and although finding 'the gap between "is" and "ought" that politics hides out' (Gates 1992, 330) may be difficult, it could be achieved by undertaking a number of specific duties.

The first duty for the academic involves the articulation of new political subjectivities, by privileging the voices of minorities and marginalised groups and mobilising politically around these. This is done by naming the groups, since, as Critchley reminds us, politics always requires naming a political subjectivity and organising around it. Ranciere usefully describes this process of naming making a discourse of that which has formerly been a noise and a process of rupture that renders certain identities visible:

> For me a political subject is a subject who employs the competence of the so-called incompetents or the part of those who have no part, and not an additional group to be recognised as part of society … It's a rupture that opens out into the recognition of the competence of anyone, not the addition of a unit. (Ranciere 2008, 3)

Critchley (2007) cites examples of 'indigenous' becoming a political force and achieving change in Mexico and Australia as a result of the process of claiming this name. In Mexico, recognising that the name 'peasant' no longer had any purchase, activists sought to enforce acceptance of a collective indigenous identity and Australian Aboriginals forcefully cemented the challenge to land rights through the establishment of a beach umbrella on the lawn facing the National Parliament which it named the 'Aboriginal Tent Embassy' (Critchley 2007, 108). Critchley advocates a kind of demonstration as demos-tration, action for the 'demos' – the people, but particularly on behalf of minorities, 'manifesting the presence of those who do not count' (2007, 130). This could be undertaken in research, writing and teaching. The dangers of patronage, of denying individuals their singular identity or of spectacularising their difference, however, are strong and should be guarded against.

A second duty involves finding a new language of civil disobedience that does not place one's own position at risk, but that nevertheless interrupts serious exchanges through the (re)introduction of the Other. This may be done through a kind of 'tactical frivolity' (Critchley 2007, 12), an example of which, on a large scale, could be seen in 'Ya Basta', in which groups dress in ridiculous, misshapen outfits, as fairies or in camp evening wear and tease riot police (by tickling them or giving them fake money to thank them for repressing dissent) or through more dialogic means. Plato takes up Socrates' notion of a particularly annoying, but persistent, gadfly:

> … if I may use such a ludicrous figure of speech, [I] am a sort of gadfly, given to the state by God; and the state is a great and noble steed who is tardy in his motions owing to his very size, and requires to be stirred into life. I am that gadfly which God has attached to the state, and all day long and in all places am always fastening upon you, arousing and persuading and reproaching you. You will not easily find another like me, and therefore I would advise you to spare me. (Plato, cited in Kraut 1992)

Whilst the image of the gadfly is seductive, I am not proposing that the academic engages in a Socratic dialogue because this is a process that is too constraining and closed. Rather, the gadfly's effect is to open up to the Other and to be ready to respond to what is forthcoming.

A third duty follows a recommendation by Torrance (2008) and is concerned with making alliances with sponsors of research and policy-makers and designing research in collaboration with, rather than on behalf of, them. It is here that the academic can introduce uncertainty into the sphere of inclusive education and research upon it and, through dialogue, can design and undertake research that is genuinely investigative. Biesta's (2008, 198) notion of 'pedagogy with empty hands', although depicting an approach to educating, is an extremely useful way of thinking about the research relationship. It requires approaching the others in the relationship without ready solutions or 'tricks of the trade', derived from research or elsewhere, and asking 'what do you think of it?' (Biesta 2008, 208). In such a relationship it will be possible to talk through 'the issues of validity, warrant, appropriateness of focus and trustworthiness of results', as Torrance (2008, 522) advocates. Academics may also be able to open sponsors' and policy-makers' eyes to the aporetic features of the educational terrain and, following Samuel Beckett, could offer, as an alternative to success criteria, frameworks for failing effectively. Such an approach has been attempted in a recent knowledge exchange activity within a programme, Sistema Scotland, which was attempting social inclusion through classical music. Presenting the policy choices to the programme managers as aporias proved difficult and uncomfortable for them but it forced them to consider how their decisions could lead to the exclusion of particular groups (Allan et al. 2010). The sociology of disability could potentially make a significant contribution through concepts, language, and in relation to thinking itself. Torrance advocates that we 'acknowledge the imperfections of what we do' (2008, 523), but these imperfections are also potentially where new ideas and possibilities for change emerge.

The final duty concerns the act of writing. Foucault suggests that to write is to 'show oneself, make oneself seen, make one's face appear before the other' (1977, 243) and, drawing on Seneca and Epictetus, views writing as a form of meditation that enables one to engage in 'work of thought', extended through the process of putting down thoughts, obtaining reactions from others and thinking and writing further. Writing could also be the main mechanism of provocation, whereby the academic, acting as the Socratic gadfly (or as Gogol's [1985] 'inky thug'), could arouse, persuade and reproach its readers to see something other than their own view of the world. Len Barton (2008a) underlines the importance of being contentious in writing, 'because it assumes there will be a necessity of struggling over ideas, arguments and interpretations ... constantly re-examining and re-thinking through these issues'. These forms of writing are worlds apart from the impact factor-driven approach to publication and the criteria for their assessment, including such elements as 'clarity' and 'coherence' in which the thinking is assumed to be complete before the article is written. Perhaps, as well as going along with these imperatives, academics need to find new outlets for writing – for example, monographs or journals with an experimental purpose, many examples of which exist in the arts, and spaces in which this is encouraged, such as Open Space (www.openspaceworld.org/) and the Laboratory of Educational Theory at the Stirling Institute of Education (www.ioe.stir.ac.uk/research/Laboratoryfor EducationalTheory.php).

The academic's function, in undertaking each of these duties, is 'to compli-cate rather than explicate' (Taylor 1995, 6), allowing them to 'approach' (Biesta 2008), rather than understand, disability, inclusive education and indeed human subjectivity. It also implies replacing understanding, which always involves tracing the partial and flawed knowledge from above, with what Taylor and Saarinen (1994) call 'interstanding', that which lies between:

> When depth gives way to surface, under-standing becomes inter-standing. To comprehend is no longer to grasp what lies beneath but to glimpse what lies between ... Understanding is no longer possible because nothing stands under ... Interstanding has become unavoidable because everything stands between. (Taylor and Saarinen 1994, 2–3)

The task of obtaining knowledge, or interstanding, about disability, according to Len Barton (2008a), involves 'challenging and removing ignorance and narrow restrictive regulatory conceptions and understandings'. Interstanding about disability is logically achieved through, and by, disabled people, and Carol Thomas (1999) advocates a narrative identity approach, in which indi-viduals' storied self-identities are set within the context of public narratives of disability, for example in the media, an approach that has parallels with 'story telling' within critical race theory (Gillborn 2008). Interstanding about inclusive education and how this might be achieved is also necessarily sought from those most closely involved with it – disabled children and their families – with insights not into techniques or 'what works' but into what makes a material difference to them and how.

The legacy of the sociology of disability, initiated by Len Barton together with other academics, both disabled and able bodied, is powerful, but is one that has not been allowed to fulfil its potential. This has partly been caused by some of the tensions and struggles within the field, which has led to a series of troubling erasures, the removal of the body within the debate on the social model of disability and the disappearance of the Other in educational policies and practices. I have argued, however, that academics within the sociology of disability have minimised their own presence within disability politics and consequently have limited their effects. The potential of the sociology of disability could be realised through a renewal of political commitment by academics and by undertaking duties that exercise responsi-bility to the Other. Such an engagement could provide academics with a much-needed revival of their professional selves by enabling them to replace concerns about accountability and audit with a desire for civic duty and for dismantling disabling and exclusionary pressures within education and soci-ety. The struggle for inclusive education would thus become one to which academics can make a significant and positive contribution by refusing to reduce it to 'quick slick responses' (Barton 2008b, 28) and helping instead to articulate the complex and difficult demands associated with becoming inclusive.

References

Allan, J. 2008. *Rethinking inclusion: The philosophers of difference in practice.* Dordrecht: Springer.

Allan, J., and R. Slee. 2008. *Doing inclusive education research.* Rotterdam: Sense.

Allan, J., N. Moran, C. Duffy, and G. Loening. 2010. Knowledge exchange with Sistema Scotland. *Journal of Education Policy* 25, no 3: 335–47.

Ballard, K. 2003. Teaching, identity and trust. In *Inclusion, participation and democracy: What is the purpose?*, ed. J. Allan, 11–32. Dordrecht: Kluwer.

Barnes, C., and G. Mercer. 2002. *Disability (key concepts).* Oxford: Blackwell Publishers.

Barnes, C., G. Mercer, and T. Shakespeare. 1999. *Exploring disability: A sociological introduction.* Cambridge: Polity Press.

Barton, L., ed. 1988. *The politics of special educational needs.* Lewes: Falmer Press.

Barton, L. 1997. Inclusive education: Romantic, subversive or realistic? *International Journal of Inclusive Education* 1, no. 3: 231–42.

Barton, L. 2001. Disability, struggle and the politics of hope. In *Disability, politics and the struggle for change,* ed. L. Barton, 1–10. London: David Fulton.

Barton, L. 2005. Special educational needs: A new look. http://www.leeds.ac.uk/disability-studies/archiveuk/barton/Warnock.pdf.

Barton, L. 2008a. Routledge interview with Professor Len Barton. Interview 5. http://www.educationarena.com/expertInterviews/interview5.asp#link2 (accessed February 26, 2010).

Barton, L. 2008b. Inclusive education, teachers and the politics of possibility. Paper presented at the Inclusion Festival, 21 January, in University of Utrecht, Holland.

Barton, L., and P. Clough. 1995. Conclusion: Many urgent voices. In *Making difficulties: Research and the construction of SEN,* ed. P. Clough and L. Barton, 143–48. London: Paul Chapman.

Barton, L., and S. Tomlinson, eds. 1984. *Special education and social interests.* London: Harper Row.

Beckett, S. 1992. *Westward ho. Nowhow on.* London: Calder.

Biesta, G. 2008. Pedagogy with empty hands: Levinas, education and the question of being human. In *Levinas and education: At the intersection of faith and reason,* ed. D. Egéa-Kuehne, 198–219. London: Routledge.

Booth, T. 2003. Views from the insititution: Overcoming barriers to inclusive education? In *Developing inclusive education,* ed. T. Booth, K. Nes and M. Strømstad, 33–58. London: RoutledgeFalmer.

Booth, T., and M. Ainscow. 1998. From them to us: Setting up the study. In *From them to us: An international study of inclusion in education,* ed. T. Booth and M. Ainscow, 1–20. London: Routledge.

Bourdieu, P. 1998. *Practical reason.* Cambridge: Polity.

Brantlinger, E. 2006. The big glossies: How textbooks structure (special) education. In *Who benefits from special education? Remediating (fixing) other people's children,* ed. E. Brantlinger, 45–76. Mahwah, NJ: Lawrence Erlbaum Associates.

Butler, J. 2004. *Precarious lives.* London: Verso.

Cohen, T. 2001. *Jacques Derrida and the humanities: A critical reader.* Cambridge: Cambridge University Press.

Corker, M. 1999. New disability discourse, the principle of optimisation and social change. In *Disability discourse,* ed. M. Corker and M. French, 192–209. Buckingham: Open University Press.

Critchley, J. 1999. *The ethics of deconstruction.* Edinburgh: Edinburgh University Press.

Critchley, J. 2007. *Infinitely demanding: Ethics of commitment, politics of resistance.* London: Verso.

Croll, P., and D. Moses. 2000. Ideologies and utopias: Education professionals' views of inclusion. *European Journal of Special Needs Education* 15, no. 1: 1–12.

Crow, L. 1992. Renewing the social model of disability. *Coalition News* July: 5–9.

Davis, L. 2002. *Bending over backwards: Disability, dismodernism and other difficult positions.* New York: New York University Press.

Derrida, J. 1990. Force of law: The mystical foundation of authority, trans. M. Quaintance. *Cardozo Law Review* 11: 919–1070.

Derrida, J. 1992. *The other heading: Reflections on today's Europe.* Trans P. Brault and M. Naas. Bloomington: Indiana University Press.

Derrida, J. 1993. *Aporias.* Stanford, CA: Stanford University Press.

Dyson, A. 2001. Special needs in the twenty-first century: Where we've been and where we're going. *British Journal of Special Education* 28, no. 1: 24–9.

Dyson, A., A. Howes, and B. Roberts. 2002. *A systematic review of the effectiveness of school-level actions for promoting participation by all students.* EPPI-Centre Review, version 1.1. Research Evidence in Education Library. London: EPPI-Centre, Social Science Research Unit, Institute of Education.

Erevelles, N. 2006. Deconstructing difference: Doing disability studies in multicultural educational contexts. In *Vital questions facing disability studies in education,* ed. S. Danforth and S. Gabel, 363–78. New York: Peter Lang.

Evans, M. 2004. *Killing thinking: The death of the universities.* London: Continuum.

Flvyberg, B. 2001. *Making social science matter: Why social inquiry fails and how it can succeed again.* Cambridge, MA: Cambridge University Press.

Foucault, M. 1977. A preface to transgression. In *Language, countermemory, practice: Selected essays and interviews by Michel Foucault,* ed. D. Bouchard, 69–86. Oxford: Basil Blackwell.

French, S. 1993. Disability, impairment or something in between. In *Disabling barriers, enabling environments,* ed. J. Swain, S. French, C. Barnes, and C. Thomas, 17–25. London: Sage.

French, S., ed. 1994. *On equal terms: Working with disabled people.* Oxford: Butterworth-Heinemann

Furedi, F. 2004. *Where have all the intellectuals gone?* London: Continuum.

Gamarnikow, E., and A. Green. 2009. Social capitalism for linking professionalism and social justice in education. In *Social capital, professionalism and diversity,* ed. J. Allan, J. Ozga, and G. Smyth, 1–20. Rotterdam: Sense.

Garrison, J. 2008. Ethical obligation in caring for the other. In *Levinas and education: At the intersection of faith and reason,* ed. D. Egéa-Kuehne, 272–85. London: Routledge.

Gates, H. 1992. Statistical stigmata. In *Deconstruction and the possibility of justice,* ed. D. Cornell, M. Rosenfield, and D. Carlson, 330–45. London: Routledge.

Gewirtz, S., and A. Cribb. 2006. What to do about values in social research: The case for ethical reflexivity in the sociology of education. *British Journal of Sociology of Education* 27, no. 2: 141–55.

Gewirtz, S., and A. Cribb. 2008. Differing to agree: A reply to Hammersley and Abraham. *British Journal of Sociology of Education* 29, no. 5: 559–62.

Gillborn, D. 2008. *Racism and education: Co-incidence or conspiracy?* Abingdon: Routledge.

Gloucestershire Special Schools Protection League. 2005. *The tide is turning on inclusion.* http://www.gsspl.org.uk/ (accessed March 3, 2005).

Gogol, N. 1985. *The government inspector.* Adapt. Adrian Mitchell. London: Heinmann.

Hammersley, M. 2008. Reflexivity for what? A resonse to Gewirtz and Cribb on the role of values in the sociology of education. *British Journal of Sociology of Education* 29, no. 5: 549–58.

Hanko, G. 2005. Towards an inclusive school culture: The 'affective curriculum'. In *Curriculum and pedagogy in inclusive education: Values into practice,* ed. M. Nind, J. Rix, K. Sheehy, and K. Simmons, 140–50. London/New York: RoutledgeFalmer/The Open University.

Hughes, B. 2009. Wounded/monstrous/abject: A critique of the disabled body in the sociological imaginary. *Disability and Society* 24, no. 4: 399–410.

Kraut, R. 1992. *Cambridge companion to Plato.* Cambridge: Cambridge University Press.

Levinas, I. 1969. *Totality and infinity.* Pittsburgh, PA: Duquesne University Press.

Levinas, I. 1996. *Basic philosophical writings,* ed. A. Perperzak, S. Critchley, and R. Bernasconi. Bloomingon: Indiana University Press.

Levinas, I. 1999. *Alterity and transcendence.* Columbia University Press: New York.

Macbeath, J., M. Galton, S. Steward, A. Macbeath, and C. Page. 2006. The costs of inclusion. Report prepared for the National Union of Teachers. http://www.teachers.org.uk/resources/pdf/CostsofInclusion.pdf (accessed September 24, 2006).

McNary, S. 2005. *What successful teachers do in inclusive classrooms.* London: Sage.

Mongon, J., D. Ford, and M. Whelan. 1982. *Special education and social control: Invisible disasters.* Boston: Routledge and Kegan Paul.

Morris, J. 1991. *Pride against prejudice: Transforming attitudes to disability.* London: The Women's Press.

Norwich, B. 2006. Dilemmas of inclusion and the future of education. In *Included or excluded? The challenge of the mainstream for some children,* ed. R. Cigman, 69–84. London: Routledge.

Oliver, M. 1996. *Understanding disability: From theory to practice.* Basingstoke: Macmillan.

Oliver, M. 1999. Final accounts and the parasite people. In *Disability discourse,* ed. M. Corker and S. French, 183–91. Buckingham: Open University Press.

Oliver, M., and C. Barnes. 1996. *Disabled people and social policy: From exclusion to inclusion.* London: Longman.

Paterson, L. 2003. The survival of the democratic intellect: Academic values in Scotland and England. *Higher Education Quarterly* 57, no. 1: 67–93.

Paterson, K., and B. Hughes. 1999. Disability studies and phenomenology: The carnal politics of everyday life. *Disability and Society* 14, no. 5: 597–611.

Paterson, K., and B. Hughes. 2000. Disabled bodies. In *The body, culture and society: An introduction,* ed. P. Hancock, B. Hughes, E. Jagger, K. Patterson, R. Russell, E. Tulle-Winton, and M. Tylor, 29–44. Buckingham: Open University Press.

Rancière, J. 2008. Jacques Rancière and indisciplinarity. An interview. *Art and Research* 2, no. 1: 1–10.

Said, E. 1994. *Representations of the intellectual.* London: Vintage.

Shakespeare, T. 2005. For whom the school bell tolls. BBC – Ouch! 11 July. http://www.bbc.co.uk/ouch/columnists/tom/270605_index.shtml (accessed July 11, 2007).

Shakespeare, T. 2006. *Disability rights and wrongs.* London: Routledge.

Shakespeare, T., and N. Watson. 1997. Defending the social model. *Disability and Society* 12, no. 2: 293–300.

Shildrick, M. 2002. *Embodying the monster: Encounters with the vulnerable self.* London: Sage.

Skrtic, T. 1995. *Disability and democracy: Reconstructing [special] education for postmodernity.* New York: Teachers College Press.

Slee, R. 1993. The politics of integration: New sites for old practices? *Disability, Handicap and Society* 8, no. 4: 351–60.

Slee, R. 2001. Inclusion in practice: Does practice make perfect? *Educational Review* 53, no. 2: 113–23.

Slee, R. 2003. Teacher education, government and inclusive schooling: The politics of the Faustian waltz. In *Inclusion, participation and democracy: What is the purpose?,* ed. J. Allan, 207–44. Dordrecht: Kluwer.

Slee, R., and J. Allan. 2001. Excluding the included: A reconsideration of inclusive education. *International Journal of Sociology of Education* 11, no. 2: 173–91.

Smyth, J. 2000. Reclaiming social capital through critical teaching. *Elementary School Journal* 110, no. 5: 491–511.

Spurgeon, N. 2006. Diversity and choice for children with complex learning needs. In *Included or excluded? The challenge of the mainstream for some children,* ed. R. Cigman, 57–65. London: Routledge.

Strathern, M. 1997. Improving ratings: Audit in the British university system. *European Review* 5, no. 3: 305–21.

Strathern, M. 2000. *Audit cultures: Anthropological studies in accountability, ethics and the academy.* London: Routledge.

Swain, J., and S. French. 2008. *Disability on equal terms.* London: Sage.

Taylor, M. 1995. Rhizomic folds of interstanding. *Tekhnema 2: Technics and Finitude* Spring. http://tekhnema.free.fr/2Taylor.htm (accessed June 27, 2003).

Taylor, M., and E. Saarinen. 1994. *Imagologies: Media philosophy.* London: Routledge.

Thomas, C. 1999. *Female forms: Experiencing and understanding disability.* Buckingham: Open University Press.

Thomas, C. 2007. *Sociologies of disability and illness: Contested ideas in disability studies and medical sociology.* London: Palgrave Macmillan.

Thomas, G. 2008. Theory and the construction of pathology. Paper presented at the American Educational Research Association, 24–28 March, in New York.

Thomas, G., and M. Vaughan. 2004. *Inclusive education: Readings and reflections.* Maidenhead: Open University Press.

Tomlinson, S. 1981. *Educational subnormality: A study in decision-making.* London: Routledge & Kegan Paul.

Tomlinson, S. 1982. *A sociology of special education.* London: Routledge & Kegan Paul.

Torrance, H. 2008. Building confidence in qualitative research: Engaging the demands of policy. *Qualitative Inquiry* 14, no. 4: 507–27.

Walford, G., D. Halpin, and B. Troyna. 1994. Political commitment in the study of the City Technology College, Kinghurst. In *Researching education policy: Ethical and methodological issues,* ed. D. Halpin and B. Troyna, 94–106. London: Falmer Press.

Warnock, M. 2005. *Special educational needs: A new look.* Impact No 11. London: The Philosophy Society of Great Britain.

Westwood, P. 2002. *Commonsense methods for children with special educational needs.* London: FalmerRoutledge.

Wing, L. 2006. Children with autistic spectrum disorders. In *Included or excluded? The challenge of the mainstream for some children,* ed. R. Cigman. London: Routledge.

A time for the universal right to education: back to basics

Marcia H. Rioux and Paula C. Pinto

School of Health Policy and Management, York University, Toronto, Ontario, Canada

The participation of children with disabilities in regular schools is too often the prerogative of education boards, who decide whether a child can learn within existing educational environments, rather than pressuring for systemic change and organization in school curricula that would grant the right of education to all children. This article looks at education as a right, as found in international agreements including the UN Covenant on Social, Economic and Cultural Rights, the UN Convention on the Rights of the Child and the UN Convention on the Rights of People with Disabilities, and education as a development tool, and discusses the limits and potential in each of these frameworks. An alternative model is proposed as an approach to *universal pedagogy*, which incorporates the idea of a flexible curriculum and the development of literacy skills, accessible and applicable to students with different backgrounds, learning styles, and abilities. Qualitative data from a large study in a number of nations monitoring the rights of people with disabilities are presented to illustrate the arguments and provide the perspective of people with disabilities themselves about their experiences in schools.

Introduction

I have argued that disability must be viewed as a form of oppression and as such it needs to be understood as part of a wider set of inequalities and oppression. The socio-political perspective adopted … provide a framework in which the voices of people with disabilities can be heard and engaged with … reminds us that current conceptions, policies and practices are neither natural nor neutral… this approach gives particular critical attention to the position and responsibilities of government and the political-will required for the development and implementation of appropriate legislation and support. (Barton 1993)

Disability and difference have largely been disregarded in the education system until very recently. There is now an emerging interest in how this has happened and how it could be remedied. Many scholars and advocates in the field of disability are looking at the systemic barriers that have justified some children not being priorities in the school system. Heightened interest in getting students with disabilities into schools is not uniform, however, and the success of integration, as it has been conducted so far, is in many instances questionable.

The simple reason for the systematic exclusion of children with disabilities from regular schools is that there has been an underlying assumption that education will not benefit a large proportion of people with disabilities (Armstrong 2007). Hence the category of uneducable, as a status, which underpinned the exclusionary policies for most of the twentieth century in many countries. The notion of mental subnormality was another amorphous categorization of children with disabilities that precluded their entry into schools. The presumption of uneducable impacted on the subsequent status of adults with disabilities as unemployable. That meant that persons with disabilities were not a focus of the employment policies either.

Literacy skills were also not a fundamental criterion for the education of many people with disabilities as there was no presumption there was a need for anything more than basic life-skills training. However, life skills were defined by those who were carers, not by people with disabilities themselves. Moreover, the common use of such developmental scales as age or IQ further diminished any presumption of need for education or literacy.

Not surprisingly, then, the literacy skills of people with disabilities have been found to remain significantly lower than others. In a recent study in Canada, for example, it was found that the rate at which people with disabilities had less than a Grade Nine education was nearly triple the rate for people without disabilities (Zubrow and Rioux 2009).

Even when, in more recent decades, inclusion has become the mantra of education systems worldwide, the discrepancy between normative frameworks and the resources available on the ground to realize the right to education for all has often created new forms of marginalization and exclusion along ability lines. Indeed, getting children with disabilities in schools is not enough. If inclusion simply changes the location of the schooling of the child but the negative stereotyping persists, then the expectations for that child's learning will continue to be less than for other students. It makes a charade of inclusion. Being 'in' a classroom, but not an integrated and equal participant in the very fabric of learning contradicts the purpose of schooling. This is what is sometimes characterized as soft inclusion – inclusion that addresses place but not the substance of learning.

A rights approach to education, by contrast, highlights the need for a holistic perspective, requiring a framework that takes into consideration not just the right of access to education throughout all stages of childhood and beyond, but also the right of quality education and the right to respect in the learning environment. In other words, it addresses 'children's rights to education, as well as rights within education' (UNICEF and UNESCO 2007, vii). Armstrong and

Barton (1999b) raise further questions related to the dilemmas of education and human rights in the following way:

> ... if schools become open and accessible to disabled students, but once admitted they are then at risk of exclusion and discriminatory treatment on the grounds of race, gender, class poverty or their status as refugees, what questions does this raise about human rights? If we see the question of human rights as concerning all members of all societies, including, of course, all children and young people –whether they go to school or not – the arguments, challenge and efforts undertaken by those involved will be more powerful and unified in terms of understanding and changing the structures and processes that exclude and oppress groups within and across different communities. (Armstrong and Barton 1999b, 3; original emphasis)

The first half of this paper presents findings that emerged from monitoring disability rights in a number of countries in both developed and developing economies. These stories provide an illustration of the experiences of people with disabilities in educational settings, collected through in-depth interviews in several countries and analyzed through the lens of human rights. Building on this empirical data, the second half of the paper outlines some key international developments in moving towards the recognition of education as a universal right, and raises issues relating to why there are still millions of people with disabilities with no access to education in 2010.

There have been a number of significant developments in the field of human rights in the past 20 years. There have also been some development initiatives that have recognized that education is fundamental to the democratization and progress of nations. Access to education in international discourse as both a rights issue and a development issue are important to getting children with disabilities into schools.

Voices of people with disabilities

The experiences of people with disabilities do not reflect an optimistic view of education as a universal right.[1] Indeed, recent studies from a number of countries suggest that people with disabilities are far from encountering an education setting in which they are welcomed and accommodated. Data from Disability Rights Promotion International (DRPI),[2] a large study that is monitoring the rights of people with disabilities in line with the standards of the Convention on the Rights of Persons with Disabilities (CRPD) and other international human rights instruments, suggest that people with disabilities are not moving forward in getting the benefits of an education, and in some cases seem to be falling further behind their peers. The following findings are drawn from individual monitoring interviews conducted in a variety of countries from the North and the South. Each interview followed a flexible guide. From an initial broad question, 'Which things have you found more satisfying in your life over the last five years? And which things have presented the greatest obstacles or barriers?', participants named two or three key situations that were used by the monitors to engage in a conversation that probed daily life experiences, assessing those experiences in relation to their conformity with general human rights principles of autonomy, dignity, inclusion participation and accessibility, equality and non-discrimination and respect for difference. The aggregate analysis of the qualitative data gathered through this process has enabled an examination of a wide range of life experiences that were coded and analyzed in seven key domains: family, work, social participation, information and communication, access to justice, income security and supports, and education.

Worldwide, a significant gap was found to persist between educational rights on paper and the enjoyment of those rights on the ground. Some of the stories collected in this study[3] describe rewarding experiences of educational inclusion and achievement by persons with disabilities. Most often, however, they provide accounts of discrimination, exclusion and disrespect, with significant consequences for the human rights, the life opportunities, the dignity and autonomy of those interviewed. While DRPI systemic analyses have highlighted some progress in legislation protecting the equal right to education of all children including those with disabilities in various countries of the world (see, for example, Philippines 2007), progress has been more impressive in principle than in practice. Figure 1, showing aggregate data from DRPI monitoring projects in four distinct sites (Bolivia, Canada, India and the Philippines), indicates that access to education for children with disabilities is often blocked by barriers in physical environments, lack of adequate supports, underfunding and prejudicial or demeaning social attitudes.

Close to 50% of all persons with disabilities interviewed in these studies specifically reported experiences of violation or denial of fundamental human rights in education. The proportion was even higher among women, suggesting gender impacts and the intersection of multiple forms of discrimination within this group. Women were found to be more prone to coercion in decisions regarding education, with many facing difficulties in getting admitted to the school or college of their choice due to their disabilities. Particularly in countries of the global South, belonging to a poor family, being a girl and a disabled child appears to serve as a powerful deterrent to further investments in education. In these and other contexts, girls who nevertheless were able to access education were also more likely than their male counterparts to be subjected to disrespectful and unequal treatment within the school system. These experiences eroded their sense of human dignity and contributed to their social isolation or even exclusion from educational settings. One participant in Bolivia, for instance, confided:

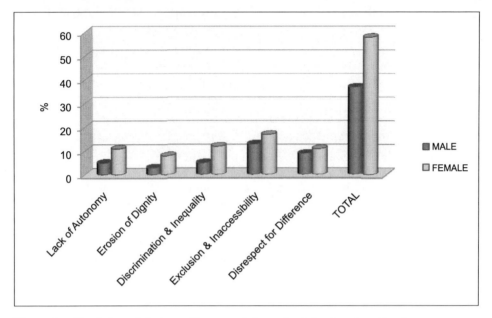

Figure 1.   Denial or violation of human rights principles in education by sex.
Source: Aggregate data from Disability Rights Promotion International Individual Monitoring Projects (Bolivia, Canada – Toronto and Quebec, India and the Philippines)

> About my education, for example I went to a hearing school but nobody paid attention to me… I didn't know what to do or who was going to help me with the homework. They didn't help me or support me at school, I felt unmotivated, bored, so that's what happened when I got into that school, and I felt really bad, and couldn't continue my studies, because… they didn't accept me as I was in a hearing school and there was nobody to help me and well afterwards I went to a school for deaf people. (Male, DRPI Bolivia)

Stories such as this clearly show that moving from human rights on paper to the enjoyment of rights in people's lives remains a challenge today for many persons with disabilities. Within a human rights approach, the disadvantages experienced by persons with disabilities are identified as human rights violations, occurring when fundamental human rights principles of *autonomy*, *dignity*, *non-discrimination*, *inclusion*, and *respect for difference* are breached and disabled persons are, as a consequence, denied equal opportunities or are prevented from achieving outcomes equal to those available to all other citizens.

Autonomy

> Well my troubles began when I graduated from high school and I couldn't get into university because of my impairment. My dream was to be a professional….

but unfortunately I couldn't because of my hearing problem because in this country there is almost no help from the professors. (Male, DRPI Bolivia)

In the context of disability, autonomy is the right of an individual to make their own choices in matters relevant to his or her life. Persons with disabilities have historically been denied this right under the presumption that disability, and particularly intellectual disability, implies the lack of capacity for moral freedom. This prevailing view has turned persons with disabilities into objects rather than subjects capable of self-directing their choices (Quinn and Degener et al. 2002). Perceived as having little to contribute to society, the education of persons with disabilities is thus often devalued – parents, teachers and school administrators decide whether a child with disability will attend school or not. The best interest of the child becomes the best interest of those around the child (Rioux et al. 2010; Barton 1997). Barriers in the physical environment and lack of adequate transportation, inadequate training of teachers or insufficient supports further reduce the educational choices available to children and youth with disabilities (UN Human Rights Council 2007). Data from DRPI monitoring projects have shown that, regardless of their will or desire, many persons with disabilities were prevented from attending school altogether; others had been coerced to attend special schools or had to take up training in specific areas deemed more appropriate to their disabilities. For example, a woman interviewed in India confided:

> No one would lift me when I was a baby because they said I was too heavy for them to lift and carry. I wanted to go to school but my elder brothers would go to work and so there was no one left to take care of me, so I dropped out of school when I was five years old. (Female, DRPI India)

Restricted in their opportunities to get a decent education, many people with disabilities were later faced with reduced employment prospects and risked poverty, as this participant in Kenya has shared:

> To me the biggest problem I have is because I was not taken to school by my parents such that I cannot access employment up to now. Though my father pretended that it was because he pitied me and had my interest at heart, I knew he was discriminating against me. Even if you have to sell vegetables you must have some little knowledge of bookkeeping. … I never had a chance to advance my studies I know my chances for employment are limited too. I feel it was due to ignorance on the part of my dad because had he allowed me to go to school, I would be better off today. (Male, DRPI Kenya)

Dignity

A rights-based approach to education implies not just rights to access to education but rights *within* education, notably the right of every child to respect for his or her inherent dignity (UNICEF and UNESCO 2007). Missing an education that prepares for adult life free from any form of abuse or violence has consequences that go far beyond economics and have an impact on the sense of worth and dignity of the person. An interviewee in India has asserted just this when he was asked how he felt about having to stop his education at an early age because of his disability:

> I really felt miserable and I thought, 'why should I live anymore, everything is a problem, it is a problem to go anywhere, to continue my education and I really am very tired of my life'. (Male, DRPI India)

Human rights are about protecting and promoting the dignity of all people. When the needs and interests of people with disabilities are ignored in the social and physical organization of the education system or when persons with disabilities are excluded from school activities on the grounds of their disability, their human dignity is hurt. This constitutes a breach of their fundamental human rights. In Bolivia, for instance, a woman and wheelchair user reported feelings of distress for having been refused admission to one school due to lack of physical accessibility in the building. Similar stories were collected in almost every country surveyed in the South. Others told us about how the lack of accessible transportation, books and materials powerfully showed them they were deemed unworthy of a public education. And while in the North discrimination was often more subtle, many people with disabilities were still found to be frustrated in their educational expectations. The demeaning treatment some of them had received in educational contexts often led them to self-destroying feelings, as this Canadian woman described:

> Sometimes I feel really sorry for myself and I pity myself and I think I'm a horrible person. I hate to be me ... ah ... umm. Often especially in a university and in an environment that is not made for people with disabilities. Umm ... so I'm constantly reminded of that ... (Female, DRPI Canada)

Participation, accessibility and inclusion

Inclusion involves organizing systems of society both public and private, to enable all people to participate fully and effectively. To achieve full participation in education, an accessible, barrier-free physical and social environment is necessary. This encompasses, among others, access to transportation; access to technology; appropriate sources of communication and media to ensure information and communication, as well as the provision of educational activities that respond to the needs, abilities and experiences of a wide range of learners (UNESCO 2008). Access to education is a universal right enshrined in the Universal Declaration of Human Rights as well as in other major international human rights treaties, including the CRPD. Nevertheless, the DRPI research has found that too often disability provides the grounds on which exclusion from education is perpetuated and legitimized. In the Philippines, for instance, an interviewee reported:

> I was rejected by the school because of my disability. It was a public school. The principal was afraid that I might figure in an accident. There was no law yet at that time. It was disheartening because you were denied your right to study in a normal school. (Male, DRPI Philippines)

The lack of domestic legislation protecting the right of all to education allows those in power to take over and make decisions that favor the *status quo* and are guided by discriminatory attitudes, prejudice and low expectations about the real abilities of people with disabilities, as this man from Cameroon has experienced:

> When I wanted to register for the maitrise level, I had to fill out some forms. My friend (who is also blind) and I went to see our teacher so that he would help us filling out those forms. But he bluntly refused to do it. He told us that he didn't want to be bothered in class, because the maitrise level is more difficult and requires a lot of mobility. And therefore having blind students in the classroom would create a lot of problems for him. (Male, DRPI Cameroon)

Yet even where such legislation exists, as in Canada, exclusion on the grounds of disability takes place, for instance, when adaptive technologies and or accessible materials are not in place, thus preventing full participation of all students. The following is an excerpt from an interview conducted in Toronto that provides a clear example of these kinds of barriers:

> Respondent: There have been several times where I have applied for continuing education courses at a fairly advanced level and have been told by the educational centres that they cannot offer this course to a blind person.
> Interviewer: What services or assistance would you need?
> Respondent: Um … the ability to adapt some of the course material …, in my particular case it was to install special software on the testing computer so I could use it …and sometimes that was the issue.
> Interviewer: Did you receive it?
> Respondent: Nope.
> Interviewer: How did that affect you?
> Respondent: Well – it's simple. It prevented me from participating. It was an absolute barrier. (Male, DRPI Canada)

Non-discrimination and equality

The principle of non-discrimination means that all rights are guaranteed to everyone, without distinction, exclusion or restriction based on disability or race, sex, language, religion, political or other opinion, national or social origin, property, birth, age, or any other status. In the context of disability, discrimination means any distinction, exclusion or restriction that has the purpose or effect of denying the recognition, enjoyment or exercise by persons with disabilities, on an equal footing, of all human rights and basic freedoms. The CRPD is unambiguous in the prohibition of all forms of discrimination on the basis of disability and explicitly calls upon states to ensure that persons with disabilities are not excluded from free and compulsory primary education, or from secondary education on the basis of disability. Article 24, dedicated to education, further establishes the right to 'reasonable accommodation' as a means to guarantee access and success in education for learners with disabilities.

In contrast with these guarantees, however, the DRPI study has confirmed that education is often a site of discrimination and inequality for people with disabilities around the world. Indeed, opportunities opened to persons with disabilities to receive an education of the same quality as that provided to other learners are often significantly diminished by the lack of adequate accommodation of their particular learning characteristics and needs, a circumstance with significant social, cultural and economic impacts in their lives. This male respondent in Kenya, who was also a teacher, for instance, reported:

> We don't have Braille books in the new syllabus and I have to rely on obsolete books. The government should plan beforehand to provide the necessary Braille course books on time. This would place blind children at par with the sighted ones. In my class, I usually have someone read the book for me, I Braille it (which takes time) and hand the children in small bits.

Given the lack of appropriate materials available to them, for both this teacher and his blind students keeping pace with the school work could not be but an added challenge, which set them to failure from the start. A standardized teaching approach can have the same impact in its failure to recognize the multitude of learning styles. This clearly places persons with disabilities at disadvantage, and thus constitutes a violation of the universal right to education. In all the countries surveyed during the pilot phase, the DRPI research gathered similar accounts of discriminatory and unequal treatment on the grounds of disability. Another participant in India for example stated:

> I have always been interested in the Sciences but apparently there is a Government Order that disabled people should not be selected and given seats for Sciences no matter how good their marks scores. I tried my level best to convince the college administration and when that failed, I met all the local political representatives and leaders and requested them to recommend to the college to include my name in the Sciences list. ... [But] the administration remained adamant ... Given these problems I had no other choice but to apply for a seat in the Commerce course and joined there. The day I joined up I felt really bad, it was because of my disability, because I do not have the use of my legs that those people refused to give me a seat in the Sciences. If I too were like the others they would not have even thought twice about my applying for that seat. I decided to join in the Commerce course because I had decided to continue my education at any cost and so had to study something, if not what I most preferred to. (Male, DRPI India)

DRPI field studies have found that disability-based discrimination is pervasive in education systems across the world, even where laws and regulations are in place to ensure equal rights to all students. Thus in Canada, for instance, while interviewees reported being granted the necessary accommodations (e.g. extra time to complete tests and assignments or accessible materials and technologies) more often than in other places, many also told about discriminatory attitudes and misconceptions of teachers school staff and peers, as this woman described:

> I was denied an application and the only reason I found that out is they called us all in through the guidance office and … hum … we went in groups of our class. And of course I was with kids that are my friends and said, 'you were ahead of me in the line you'd go in and get the application, I'd go in after you'. And all of a sudden they didn't have any, and the person who went in after me got one. And then we'd go out in the hall and I'd think: 'you were lined after me and they told me they ran out of them', you know, and then I'd realize the guidance counsellor was making a value judgement saying that in her mind she didn't think that I warranted the opportunity, because she didn't think I could do it. (Female, DRPI Canada)

The constant discrediting of their learning abilities and their methods of learning that people with disabilities so often face is a form of discrimination that fosters exclusion along disability lines. Once internalized it leads to lowered self-expectations on the part of students with disabilities themselves, affecting the students' productivity and academic proficiency. In this sense, it also denotes disrespect for the person and for disability as an expression of the human diversity, which constitutes a fundamental tenet of the rights approach.

Respect for difference

In human rights theory and practice, respect for difference involves acceptance of persons with disabilities as part of human diversity and humanity. Despite visible or less apparent differences, all people have the same rights and dignity. In educational settings all are entitled to respect for their identity and integrity (UNICEF and UNESCO 2007). A rights-based perspective in education demands that the best interest of the child always prevail and inform the provision of quality education that empowers all children. The inclusion of narratives and images of disability in the texts of history, social science literature, and so on, for instance, can provide important means of social and cultural recognition. Their more typical absence, on the contrary, conveys the unspoken message that disability is not considered an integral normative experience. Thus to ensure respect for all in and through education, the responsibility to change falls not on the individual but on the school system that must accept a diversity of learners and be responsive to their different abilities and needs.

Results from DRPI studies across all countries and world regions show that there is still a long way to go to achieve such a goal. Many persons with disabilities interviewed for this research reported experiences of harassment and disrespect in school environments, including labeling on the basis of disability, teasing and mocking or name-calling. A woman in Cameroon, for instance, confided: 'One time I was walking in the school yard and I heard one of my peers saying: "look how she walks, the disabled"'. Another one in the Philippines recalled the embarrassment she used to feel during school performances when her speech impairment was the cause of mockery and imitation by other students. But disrespect for disability was not always conveyed in obvious forms. More subtle forms of disrespect similarly suggest an unwillingness to accommodate and respond to the diverse characteristics of learners with disabilities, as this interviewee in Cameroon has shared:

> There are certain teachers who do not understand the importance of education for blind people. Sometimes they misplace our essays when they are marking them, since our writing is different from other students'. Despite our efforts, some of them behave as if our presence disrupts the good working of the university. (Female, DRPI Cameroon)

Negative attitudes such as these, and general inattention to the educational characteristics of learners with disabilities are perhaps more difficult to change by decree. They require strong policies that emphasize disability-awareness training at all societal levels and a real commitment to human rights at all levels of education planning and delivery.

Education and human rights: why the gap?

The right to education was given formal recognition in the 1948 Universal Declaration on Human Rights (United Nations 1948). It was also articulated in the International Covenant on Economic, Social and Cultural Rights (United Nations 1966), which asserts:

1. The States Parties to the present Covenant recognize the right of everyone to education. They agree that education shall be directed to the full development of the human personality and the sense of its dignity, and shall strengthen the respect for human rights and fundamental freedoms. They further agree that education shall enable all persons to participate effectively in a free society, promote understanding, tolerance and friendship among all nations and all racial, ethnic or religious groups, and further the activities of the United Nations for the maintenance of peace.
2. The States Parties to the present Covenant recognize that, with a view to achieving the full realization of this right:
   (a) Primary education shall be compulsory and available free to all;
   (b) Secondary education in its different forms, including technical and vocational secondary education, shall be made generally available and accessible to all by every appropriate means, and in particular by the progressive introduction of free education;
   (c) Higher education shall be made equally accessible to all, on the basis of capacity, by every appropriate means, and in particular by the progressive introduction of free education;

(d) Fundamental education shall be encouraged or intensified as far as possible for those persons who have not received or completed the whole period of their primary education;

(e) The development of a system of schools at all levels shall be actively pursued, an adequate fellowship system shall be established, and the material conditions of teaching staff shall be continuously improved.

These instruments, however, did not enumerate any groups to which they particularly applied. The increasing pressure by families, self-advocates and disability rights groups beginning in the 1980s has influenced the move towards education for all and universal education and an increasing acceptance of these ideals, at least in theory. At the same time, there has been a growth in research in questions related to the meaning of integrated education, inclusive education, the factors that are barriers or influencers of education for all; special education, quality of education in special classes or school, the categorization of children, and the re-evaluation of the notion of special needs and school response (Alur and Rioux 2009; Rioux 2006; Allan 2008; Slee 1998; Slee and Allan 2001; Thomas and Loxley 2001; Armstrong and Barton 1999a; Barton 1995a, 1995b). Gradually, the vision of education as right, as an entitlement rather than a benefit that children with disabilities could claim, has also been introduced (Armstrong and Barton 1999b).

Key international instruments, conferences and reports have both influenced and reflected these emerging concerns and considerations, repositioning education for children with disabilities and life-long learning as issues of rights and equality. For instance, the Convention on the Rights of the Child 1989 outlined the right to education in Articles 28 and 29. Article 23 specifically recognized children with 'physical or mental' disabilities, and framed their entitlement as the right to enjoy a 'full and decent life' in conditions that ensure dignity, promote self-reliance and facilitate the child's active participation in the community. Furthermore, in General Comment No. 9, the UN Committee on the Rights of the Child (2007) specifically adopted inclusive education as the goal of educating disabled students.

The UN Decade of Disabled Persons from 1983 to 1992 provided a fertile environment to highlight the situation of people with disabilities and led to a greater recognition of the right to education for children with disabilities. In 1993, the United Nations established the 'Standard Rules on the Equalization of Opportunities for Persons with Disabilities' (Standard Rules), which included the notion of 'integrated' education (Rule 6. Education) for students with disabilities (UN Enable 2010):

- States should recognize the principle of equal primary, secondary and tertiary educational opportunities for children, youth and adults with disabilities, in integrated settings. They should ensure that the education of persons with disabilities is an integral part of the educational system.

- General educational authorities are responsible for the education of persons with disabilities in integrated settings. Education for persons with disabilities should form an integral part of national educational planning, curriculum development and school organization.
- Education in mainstream schools presupposes the provision of ... appropriate support services.
- In States where education is compulsory it should be provided to girls and boys with all kinds and all levels of disabilities, including the most severe.
- To accommodate educational provisions for persons with disabilities in the mainstream, States should:
  - Have a clearly stated policy, understood and accepted at the school level and by the wider community;
  - Allow for curriculum flexibility, addition and adaptation;
  - Provide for quality materials, ongoing teacher training and support teachers.
- Integrated education and community-based programmes should be seen as complementary approaches in providing cost-effective education and training for persons with disabilities.
- In situations where the general school system does not yet adequately meet the needs of all persons with disabilities, special education may be considered. It should be aimed at preparing students for education in the general school system.

The Standard Rules on the Equalization of Opportunities for Persons with Disabilities (United Nations 1993) are not a binding international agreement, thus there is no enforcement mechanism. However, they did lay out principles that have been influential in the movement towards inclusive education and, more importantly, a broader recognition of the purpose of education. The drawback, however, was that they provided for school boards and Ministries of Education to be decision-makers about who could most appropriately be provided special education if their current programs could not accommodate students with disabilities.

In 1994, the United Nations' Educational, Cultural and Scientific Organization (UNESCO) along with Spain's Ministry of Education and Science held a seminal meeting in Salamanca, Spain, on inclusive and special education (UNESCO and Ministry of Education Spain 1994). The Education for All Conference was a turning point in terms of recognition that all children, particularly those with disabilities, should be in school.

The Framework for Action on Special Needs Education, adopted at Salamanca, laid out a framework that specified it is the responsibility of individual schools to accommodate all children, independent of physical, intellectual, social, emotional, linguistic or any other conditions (UNESCO and Ministry of Education for Spain 1994). The vision of the accommodation of all children was that it 'should include disabled and gifted children, street and working children, children from remote or nomadic populations, children from linguistic, ethnic or cultural minorities and children from other disadvantaged or marginalized areas or groups' (UNESCO and Ministry of Education for Spain 1994, 6). Thus importantly the Declaration of Salamanca re-conceptualized the notion of participation in schools. It did this by moving away from the idea of integration in which supports are given to individual students to enable inclusion towards an understanding that the system has to be transformed so that a diversity of children learning styles can be accommodated.

In sum, the Salamanca Statement and Framework that came out of that meeting (UNESCO and Ministry of Education Spain 1994) highlighted the need for inclusive education systems and provided a guide for governments to follow in making changes towards the inclusive ideal, arguing that 'regular schools with this inclusive orientation are the most effective means of combating discriminatory attitudes, creating welcoming communities, building an inclusive society ...' (6).

Yet, while the Salamanca Statement and Framework recognized the presumption of inclusive education as an ideal, at the same time it continued to relegate some children to special settings, when it proposed to 'adopt as a matter of law or policy the principle of inclusive education, enrolling all children in regular schools, unless there are compelling reasons for doing otherwise' (UNESCO and Ministry of Education Spain 1994, 8).

A few years later, the Dakar Framework for Action (UNESCO 2000) – reaffirming the World Declaration on Education for All (UNESCO 1990) which followed the Universal Declaration on Human Rights and the Convention on the Rights of the Child – placed a new emphasis on education as a right, stating that all children have the 'human right to benefit from an education that will meet their basic leaning needs ... in the best and fullest sense of the term... It is an education geared to tapping each individual's talents and potential ...' (UNESCO 2000, 8).

In 2006 the CRPD was adopted by the United Nations, coming into force on 10 May 2008 (United Nations 2006). It makes very specific recommendations on education from its preamble in which there is recognition of the 'importance of accessibility to ... education...' through to a number of articles that recognize education in various contexts. For example, Article 8 mandates the education system at all levels to foster 'an attitude of respect for the rights of persons to disabilities', and Article 24 recognizes a general right to education for all persons with disabilities. The CRPD states that all education systems should be inclusive at all levels regardless of the student's severity of disability, making unambiguous that education is a right for persons with disabilities. Other articles in the CRPD relevant to education include Article 3 (General principles), Article 5 (Equality and non-discrimination), Article 6 (Women with disabilities), Article 7 (Children with disabilities), Article 8

(Awareness-raising), Article 9 (Accessibility) and articles that affect access to education, such as right to health, right to work, and so forth.

It is in fact, increasingly recognized today that:

> education is both a human right in itself and an indispensable means of realizing other human rights. It enables children and young people to develop a sense of their own worth and respect for others. In doing so, it fosters their ability to contribute and participate fully in their communities. (New Zealand Human Rights Commission/Tekathui Tiak Tangata 2009, 3)

The exclusion of children with disabilities from school or their discriminatory treatment in the education system is thus recognized to impact their opportunities and available resources throughout the lifecycle. Importantly too, exclusionary or disrespectful practices towards children with different levels of abilities in school are viewed as having consequences not just for these students but for all learners. Deprived from the early experience of respectfully dealing with and accepting disability as part of human diversity, nondisabled children will more probably become adults who will themselves reproduce, instead of combating, prejudicial and discriminatory practices towards persons with disabilities and their place in society.

A number of recent legal decisions[4] have also framed education as a right rather than a service for people with disabilities. However, this right has in some cases been circumscribed by devolving the decision-making to individual boards or schools, thus making it a procedural right rather than a substantive right. This has important consequences for the imperative on governments to put in place inclusive education and may indeed endanger the principle of universal education (i.e. education that is accessible to all children and adults).

Using human rights as a framework means addressing the economic, social and environmental factors and not just the access to schools. It requires addressing the barriers to inclusion and participation found in pedagogical theory, access to places of learning, capacity testing and success measuring tools and strategies. Equity in education is a commitment of the public education system to social justice. The radical reform that is needed to overcome barriers to social and economic disadvantage has to include social action that removes gender inequality, illiteracy, disability discrimination and barriers to schooling. These are important issues because they address the overbearing technological and pedagogical theories that are entrenched in the fundamental ideas about education and the capacities of people with disabilities. These have become the evidence base to judge the capacity of children to learn and the ability of people to participate in current education systems (Rioux 2006).

Education and development

Within the context of development, access to quality education is often framed as a pre-requisite for successful development. Amartya Sen, for instance, has argued that, 'Since participation requires basic educational skills, denying the opportunity to schooling to any group ... is immediately contrary to the basic conditions to participatory freedom' (Sen 2002).

From the development perspective, the benefits of basic education are argued to be greater than the individual benefit enjoyed by the person who is educated. In this sense, education ceases to be just about reading and writing to become a necessary condition for economic growth and prosperity within a nation. We are thus seeing competing agendas within international frameworks:

> For governments, there are two major goals in funding education: to develop the economic workforce and potential future wealth; and to promote social cohesion, integration and a sense of national identity. Indeed, the development of mass education during the 20th century is recognized to have played an important role in promoting national integration and uniformity in both industrialized countries and the developing world. [In contrast] a rights-based understanding of education moves beyond the more traditional model of schooling, which has defined the education agenda very much from the perspective of the government by emphasizing training human capital investment, and containment of young people and their socialization. (UNICEF and UNESCO 2007, 20)

The largest current international agenda of the development community is the achievement of the Millennium Development Goals (MDGs)[5] (United Nations 2000). There are eight goals, the second of which addresses education: 'Ensure that by 2014, children everywhere, boys and girls alike will be able to complete a full course of primary schooling'. The MDGs do not make an explicit reference to people with disabilities, but in a recent report from an Expert Group meeting organized by the Secretariat for the CRPD of the United Nations, recognition was given to the place of people with disabilities in achieving the MDGs. The Expert Group recommended mainstreaming disability into the development goals, recognizing that all MDGs are '... relevant to and affect the lives of persons with disabilities' (UN Expert Working Group 2009). They concluded that development cannot be looked at outside the context of a human-rights-based approach and its core elements.

Indeed, as stated in a 2008 paper put out by the High Commissioner on Human Rights, education is more than an exercise in furthering economic growth. Advancing a human rights approach to the MDGs, this report emphasized the importance of equitable access to education, specifically bringing into focus the 'more than 40 million children denied schooling [who] have a disability' (UN High Commissioner for Human Rights 2008, 23). It stressed the need for '... stronger attention to ensure that children with disabilities have access to the necessary educational facilities and support staff', in light of the findings that some countries have reported the fulfillment of this MDG without having provided education for children with disabilities (UN High Commissioner for Human Rights 2008, 23). Finally, the report calls for the removal of barriers that prevent children with disabilities from attending school and from getting all the incumbent benefits from education.

Alston (2009) has also argued that there are advantages for the MDG campaign to build upon the legal obligations already undertaken by governments, which have ratified human rights treaties. Particularly in the area of disability, the CRPD provides the potential for mobilization in using the rights discourse as well as the recognition of the principles of the Convention (dignity, equality, non-discrimination, and respect for difference) as powerful incentives for the development agenda to adopt a rights perspective. In addition, the monitoring mechanisms in the Convention and its Optional Protocol open new avenues for contributing to determining whether development goals as well as rights goals are being met. This may be furthered by the meeting starting on 5 October 2009 of the Third Committee of the UN General Assembly at its 64th session, to discuss disability under two agenda items: social development (Agenda Item 63(b)), and human rights (Agenda Item 71(a)).

A broader approach

While special education has held a kind of aura for encouraging the education of children with disabilities, it is grounded in the labeling of difference and a model of disability as an individual pathology (Rioux 2003). In the attempt to give students the individualized instruction they deserve, special education has had the consequence of isolating children in separate classrooms, separate schools or with special measures in regular classrooms. Children are labeled both on the basis of their capacity to learn within the context of the schools and the learning environment and the applied teaching methodology. Despite that, the arguments for special learning are still very much the currency of schools in many countries of both the North and the South. In the past 25 years a new more diverse terminology has entered the field of education and disability, including such concepts as cascade model of education, integration, inclusion, and universal pedagogy and others. There does not seem to be any precise meaning to these terms or the way in which they converge and differ with each other both in their meaning and in their application. The critical evaluation and restructuring of pedagogy is still in its infancy, perhaps not so much because it is so technically difficult but because of the complexity of taking on the education industry, the class structure and 'patriarchal, utilitarian and segregational tradition' (Munoz 2007) on which it is based. More important is the lack of a clear grounding in each of these ideas that explicitly spells out an *a priori* right to education – a right that supersedes ability or disability, individual capacity to learn and the capacity of schools to teach the diversity of students found in classroom – and a way of monitoring that right independent of the methodology applied.[6] The how-to of educational innovation that will result in children with disabilities getting an education may be accomplished by a variety of methodologies; what is essential is that it meets the basic criteria of a right to education (Peters, Johnstone, and Ferguson 2005).

Measuring achievement

The four broad international standards for determining the extent to which a right has been achieved are availability, accessibility, acceptability and adaptability (New Zealand Human Rights Commission/Tekathui Tiak Tangata 2009, 5). In a recent report, the New Zealand Human Rights Commission/ Tekathui Tiak Tangata found in an analysis of their complaints that there were significant outstanding issues for disabled students in all four components of the right to education, including:

- Availability – there is an insufficient number of people skilled and qualified as inclusive educators and/or with special education training
- Accessibility – participation rates of disabled students are disproportionately low
- Acceptability – education standards vary considerably for disabled students and the school environment is not always a safe one for them and
- Adaptability – education provision does not reasonably accommodate disabled students so that they can achieve equitable outcomes. Achievement rates for these students are disproportionately low. (New Zealand Human Rights Commission/Tekathui Tiak Tangata 2009, 10)

Each of these raises significant, complex and probing questions for inclusion and universal pedagogy. As data presented earlier in this paper showed, these remain challenging areas for students with disabilities all over the world. Inclusion is, ultimately, political (Barton 1995a). The term itself tends to apply to people with disabilities and consequently gets used as an exercise for labeling, excluding and sanitizing (Barton 2004). The struggle for inclusion is a struggle for much broader social justice – moving away from categories of people who are judged to be 'failures' within the school system – and towards institutional practices – universal learning – that accommodate the diversity of children in the schools. Allan (2008) refers to the cycle of changing words in order to continue with the 'same maledictory practices' that give the illusion of change without effect.

Universal pedagogy has adopted the concept of universal design (for example, Mace, Hardie, and Place 1996; Peterson 1999; Preiser and Ostroff 2000) to apply to learning. It incorporates the idea of a curriculum that includes alternatives to make it accessible and applicable to students with different backgrounds, learning styles, and abilities. The Victorian government in Australia emphasized in a 2007 report the importance of shifting the pedagogical focus from adaptations for special need to universal design (Australia, Department of Education, Employment and Workplace Relations 2007). Universal pedagogy addresses the key issues that are raised when human rights principles are integral to the design, implementation and evaluation of education policies and programs.

Conclusion

The gap between the international commitments to ensure that all children get educated without exclusion and the reality of educating children with disabilities in their communities still remains to be addressed. It continues to be a slow process for the recognition of the right to education for children with disabilities to become accepted and implemented. Rights of people with disabilities are in a new phase and these rights mandate a different way of perceiving education and learning, not as a pragmatic economic exercise but as the basis for engaging in society. Policies that frame education as a right but devolve the decision-making to individual boards or schools, or that promote access to education not as value in itself but as a pre-requisite for economic development, have resulted in many children with disabilities being left out or lagging behind in school systems worldwide.

The struggle for the participation of people with disabilities in all aspects of their societies arguably starts with basic education and literacy skills that are shared with non-disabled students. There is an urgent need to monitor the systemic conditions that have led to the discrepancy between policy and practice, between theory and implementation. There is a further need to disaggregate data in order to make visible the discrimination and exclusion of many children with disabilities, to develop new policies that target people with disabilities and to measure the progress towards universal education. It is time that children with disabilities are treated to the advantage of learning, through the implementation of educational innovation that recognizes the diversity of children in any classroom and encourages and rewards universal pedagogy that accommodates a variety of learning styles and needs. The basics of education were originally reading, writing and knowledge of citizenship. It is time to move back to these ideals to make sure that with appropriate support and accommodation of those becomes the right of all children without exception, in every school of the twenty-first century.

Notes

1. On 13 October 2009, the European Committee of Social Rights found violations of the right to education (Article 17(2)) and the right to non-discrimination (Article E) in Bulgaria. The decision in the case of *Mental Disability Advocacy Centre v. Bulgaria* criticized the Bulgarian government for depriving children with disabilities of education (Mental Disability Advocacy Centre 13 October 2008. www.mdac/info).
2. Launched in 2002, DRPI is a collaborative project monitoring disability discrimination globally. The project has been piloted in a number of countries of the North and the South, encompassing two broad areas of rights monitoring – 'systems' monitoring involving the collection and analyses of domestic law and public policy with impact on the lives of people with disabilities, and 'individual' monitoring through face-to-face in-depth interviews with persons of adult age with various kinds of disabilities. Read more about this project and access country reports online (http://www.yorku.ca/drpi/).

3. In every country monitored, approximately 100 interviews have been carried out. Interviews were conducted by trained monitors who are themselves persons with disabilities; each took on average two and a half hours. To guarantee that the sample is made up of representative proportions of the relevant subset of individuals in the population we are studying, DRPI defined the following four relevant dimensions to consider in each monitoring study: types of disability, gender, age, and socioeconomic status.

4. See the forthcoming Rioux et al. (2010). See also, for example, cases where the right was narrowly defined: New Zealand, *Daniels v. Attorney-General* (3 April 2002) HC AK M1516/SW99 and *Attorney General v. Daniels* (2003) 2 NZLR 742 (CA); Canada, the Eaton case; and Australia, the Purvis case.

5. The MDGs are eight goals to be achieved by 2015 that respond to the world's main development challenges. The MDGs are drawn from the actions and targets contained in the Millennium Declaration that was adopted by 189 nations and signed by 147 heads of state and governments during the UN Millennium Summit in September 2000.

6. In the report of Human Rights Council, 4th Session, 2007, Special Rapporteur Vernor Munoz held that the concept of 'inclusive education' is a 'main characteristic of the right to education' (UN Human Rights Council 2007, introduction).

References

Allan, J. 2008. *Rethinking inclusive education: The philosophers of difference in Practice*. Dordrecht, The Netherlands: Springer.

Alston, P. 2009. A human rights perspective on the Millennium Development Goals. Paper prepared as a contribution to the work of the Millennium Project Task Force on Poverty and Development, Center for Human Rights and Global Justice, NYU School of Law, New York.

Alur, M., and M. Rioux. 1999. *Included: An exploration of six early education pilot projects for children with disabilities in India*. Mumbai, India: NRCI. http://www.atkinson.yorku.ca/cdis/included.htm.

Armstrong, F. 2007. Disability, education and social change in England since 1960. *History of Education* 36, nos 4–5: 551–68.

Armstrong, F., D. Armstrong, and L. Barton, eds. 1999. *Inclusive education: Policy, contexts and comparative perspectives*. London: Fulton Books.

Armstrong, F., and L. Barton, eds. 1999a. *Difference and difficulty: Insights, issues and dilemmas*. Sheffield: Department of Educational Studies.

Armstrong, F., and L. Barton, eds. 1999b. *Disability, human rights and education: Cross cultural perspectives*. Buckingham: Open University Press.

Australia, Department of Education and Early Childhood Development. 2007. Best start – student wellbeing – health and wellbeing. http://www.education.vic.gov.au/healthwellbeing/wellbeing/beststart.htm.

Barton, L. 1993. Inaugural lecture, University of Sheffield. http://www.leeds.ac.uk/disability-studies/archiveuk/barton/inaugral%20lecture%20barton.pdf.

Barton, L. 1995a. The politics of education for all. *Support for Learning* 10: 156–60.

Barton, L. 1995b. Segregated special education: Some critical observations. In *Removing disabling barriers,* ed. G. Zarb, 27–37. London: Policy Studies Institute.

Barton, L. 1997. The politics of special educational needs. In *Disability studies: Past present and future,* ed. L. Barton and M. Oliver, 138–59. Leeds: The Disability Press,

Barton, L. 2004. Politics of special education: A necessary or irrelevant approach? In *Ideology and the politics of in/exclusion,* ed. L. Ward. New York: Peter Lang.

Mace, R.L., G.J. Hardie, and J.P. Place. 1996. *Accessible environments: Toward universal design.* Raleigh: North Carolina State University. http://www.design.ncsu.edu/cud/pubs_p/docs/ACC%20Environments.pdf.

Munoz, V. 2007. The right to education: Report of the special rapporteur on the right to education. UN General Assembly, Human Rights Council Fourth Session, Item 2 on Agenda, March 2006. http://www.internationaldisabilityalliance.org/wp-content/uploads/2009/09/Report-on-persons-with-disabilities-by-SR-on-right-to-education.pdf.

New Zealand Human Rights Commission/Tekathui Tiak Tangata. 2009. *Disabled children's right to education.* New Zealand: Human Rights Commission.

Peters, S.J., C. Johnstone, and P. Ferguson. 2005. A disability rights in education model for evaluating inclusive education. *International Journal of Inclusive Education* 9, no. 2: 139–60.

Peterson, M.J. 1999. *Gracious spaces, universal design in the home.* New York: McGraw Hill.

Philippines. 2007. Magna Carta for disabled persons: An Act providing for the rehabilitation, self-development and self-reliance of disabled persons and their integration into the mainstream of society and for other purposes. Republic Act No. 7277. Signed into law April 30.

Preiser, W., and E. Ostroff, eds. 2000. *Universal design handbook.* New York: McGraw Hill.

Quinn, G., and T. Degener, with A. Bruce, C. Burke, J. Castellino, P. Kenna, U. Kilkelly, and S. Quinlivan. 2002. *The current use and future potential of United Nations human rights instruments in the context of disability.* New York: Office of the United Nations High Commissioner for Human Rights.

Rioux, M. 2003. On second thought: Constructing knowledge, law, disability and inequality. In *The human rights of persons with intellectual disabilities: Different but equal,* ed. S. Herr, L. Gostin, and H. Koh, 287–317. Oxford: Oxford University Press.

Rioux, M. 2006. Special education needs: A legal right? In *Handbook of special education,* ed. L. Florian, 107–16. London: Sage Books.

Rioux, M., L. Basser, and M. Jones, eds. 2010, forthcoming. *Key cases in disability law.* The Hague: Brille Publishers.

Sen, A. 2002. *Rationality and freedom.* Cambridge, MA: Belknap Press of Harvard University Press.

Slee, R. 1998. The politics of theorising special education. In *Theorising special education,* ed. C. Clarke, A. Dyson and A. Millward, 30–41. London: Routledge.

Slee, R., and J. Allan. 2001. Excluding the included: A reconsideration of inclusive education. *International Journal of Sociology of Education* 11, no. 2: 173–91.

Thomas, G., and A. Loxley. 2001 *Deconstructing special education and constructing inclusion.* Buckingham: Open University Press.

UN Committee on the Rights of the Child. 2007. General Comment 9: The rights of children with disabilities. http://www.unhchr.ch/tbs/doc.nsf/%28Symbol%29/CRC.C.GC.9.En (accessed September 30, 2009).

UNESCO. 1990. *World declaration on education for all.* Paris: UNESCO.

UNESCO. 2000. *Education for all, Dakar framework for action.* France: UNESCO.

UNESCO. 2008. *Inclusive education: The way of the future.* International Conference on Education. Final Report. Geneva: UNESCO.

UNESCO and Ministry of Education Spain. 1994. The Salamanca Statement and Framework for action on special needs education. Adopted by the World Conference on Special Needs Education, 7–10 June, in Salamanca, Spain.

UN Enable. 2010. Standard rules on the equalization of opportunities for persons with disabilities. http://www.un.org/esa/socdev/enable/dissre00.htm.

UN Expert Working Group. 2009. Mainstreaming disability in MDG policies, processes and mechanisms development for all. Report of the Expert Group Meeting Organized by the Secretariat for the Convention on the Rights of Persons with Disabilities, Division for Social Policy and Development, Department of Economic and Social Affairs in collaboration with the World Health Organization, 14–16 April, in World Health Organization Headquarters, Geneva, Switzerland.

UN High Commissioner For Human Rights. 2008. *Claiming the Millennium Development Goals: A human rights approach.* Geneva: United Nations. http://www.un.org/disabilities/default.asp?id=1470.

UN Human Rights Council. 2007. The right to education for persons with disabilities: Report of the Special Rapporteur on the right to education, Venor Muñoz. http://www.un.org/Docs/journal/asp/ws.asp?m=A/HRC/4/29 (accessed September 30, 2009).

UNICEF and UNESCO. 2007. *A human rights-based approach to education for all: A framework for the realization of children's right to education and rights within education.* New York: UNICEF.

United Nations. 1948. The universal declaration of human rights. http://www.un.org/en/documents/udhr/ (accessed October 1, 2009).

United Nations. 1966. *International covenant on economic, social and cultural rights.* New York: United Nations.

United Nations. 1993. Standard rules on the equalization of opportunities for persons with disabilities. http://www.un.org/esa/socdev/enable/dissre00.htm.

United Nations. 2000. Millennium Development Goals. http://www.undp.org/mdg/.

United Nations. 2006. Convention on the rights of persons with disabilities. http://www.un.org/disabilities/convention/conventionfull.shtml.

Zubrow, E., and M. Rioux. 2009. *Landscape of literacy and disability.* Toronto: Canadian Abilities Foundation.

Response

I am delighted that a special issue of the *British Journal of Sociology of Education* has been given to an examination of Disability and Inclusive Education. The authors of the papers have all made important contributions to the advancement of knowledge and understanding in these fields of study. Overall, they have provided a comprehensive, valuable series of informed insights into a range of important ideas, issues, questions and agendas for future developments. They have also provided a relevant resource of references for readers to further explore.

When thinking about any personal contributions to these concerns, I am clearly reminded, on the one hand, of the limited nature of such work and how little effective conceptual, theoretical, empirical and applied nature of such understanding has been achieved, and, on the other, how much work still needs to be undertaken for real changes to be realised and maintained. It is also essential that one's work is always to be understood in the context of the centrality of solidarity, critical friendships and supportive networks. The privilege, challenge and benefit of working with so many wonderful colleagues, both within the Academy and outside it, have been of crucial significance in my experience.

In this brief response, I will not seek to comment on particular papers, but rather offer a selection of concerns that have been reinforced for me in the reading of these papers, and are part of the urgent tasks that need to be seriously and critically explored.

Historically, the question of disability has been a seriously neglected topic of sociological investigation. It has also been conceived in largely limited ways, in terms of merely a 'bolt-on-factor' to the more dominant forms of significant factors such as class, race, gender and sexuality. This reflects a tokenistic, superficial perspective and one that needs to be the subject of critical analysis. Another way of thinking that needs to be recognised and challenged is one that separates disability from all other forms of oppression, exclusion and discrimination, and is thus viewed as a single-issue factor. This is counter-productive to recognising and understanding the complex and interconnected nature of the varied forms of discrimination that need to be challenged and changed. In both these cases, the seriousness of the issues involved are contingent upon the degree of commitment to human rights based policy and practice.

In their endeavours to challenge the continual realities of discrimination and exclusion, including seeking to develop more inclusive conditions, thinking and relations, disabled people have developed a language of possibility through which they can express their concerns and interests. An example of such language is the concept 'struggle'. Several important assumptions inform the meaning and use of such an important metaphor. First, it signifies their understanding of the seriousness and stubborn nature of the issues involved and their real impact on the quality of their daily lives. Secondly, it highlights the difficult, challenging nature of the perennial engagement with these barriers and the development and maintenance of alternative thinking, understanding and practices. Finally, such language encourages increasing awareness and understanding that there are no quick, slick, easy solutions to what are fundamental issues.

The social model of disability

If we want to take seriously the question of disability, then it is absolutely necessary that we give priority to the voices of disabled people. With regard to the development and application of policies, programmes and decision-making that will affect the quality of their lives, the disability movement has a clear message which is 'Nothing About Us Without Us'. They need to be actively involved in such developments and practices. In seeking to provide alternative insights, definitions and agendas in opposition to the disabling world they daily experience, they have created a tool that has become known as 'The Social Model of Disability'. This is not an uncontested development and is the subject of critical examination by disabled people as well as other parties. The model has served several functions, including providing a framework and language through which disabled people themselves can describe their experiences. Discrimination, exclusion and inequality can be named and challenged. Also, it offers a means through which the question of disability can be explored and understood in terms of wider socio-economic conditions and relations. This is in contrast to individualised, deficit conceptions and understandings. It also provides a basis for support, encouragement and collective endeavours of disabled people. Finally, it is a means through which the non-disabled world can be provided with alternative, positive views of disability. Thus it has a very important educative function (Barton 2003).

Whilst recognising and discussing some of the main challenges that have been made against the social model, Barnes (2003) provides a clear message as to the central purpose of its development:

> It is a concerted attempt to *politicize* disability in order to provide a clear and unambiguous focus on the very real and multiple deprivations that are imposed on people whose biological conditions are deemed socially unacceptable in order to bring about radical, structural and cultural change. (Barnes 2003, 19)

Not only does he seek to challenge those who maintain that the social model denies the importance of issues relating to the body and psycho-emotional, concerns that incidentally he himself is daily reminded of as a disabled person, he also reinforces the centrality of this approach in the struggle for a non-oppressive, non-discriminatory world.

The social model encourages a priority to be given to identifying and critiquing all those individualistic, deficit, sentimentalising, exclusionary assumptions and beliefs, which have informed and continue to inform discriminatory policies and practices. It also goes beyond the issue of disablement and is about the establishment and maintenance of a social world, in which all people experience the realities of inclusive values and relationships in their daily lives. Hence, there needs to be a zero-tolerance with regard to all forms of discrimination and exclusion. A topic that needs much more serious examination and analysis concerns the issue of the inter-connection of multiple forms of discrimination, including simultaneous forms of oppression, as well as highlighting points of commonality and difference.

Globalisation

The question of disability and inclusion becomes a more complex, contentious and challenging issue when placed within the context of a cross-cultural global dimension. Global changes are not experienced equally or in the same way by different societies. Starved of resources, constrained by the legacies of colonialism and experiencing forms of dependency through the political and economic dominance of more powerful minority world countries of the North, the damaging impact of policy-borrowing and the imposition of forms of discourse, policies and programmes of action, supported by various aid packages, have become a reality in the majority world countries of the South (Armstrong, Armstrong, and Spandagou 2010). These developments created in different geographical and social contexts lacked serious, sensitive, respectful understanding of the history, culture and socio-religious dimensions of the majority world societies involved. Thus, key concepts such as 'social justice' and 'inclusion' are used in an uncritical manner as if they have a universal meaning and application (Alur and Timmons 2009; Connell 2007).

Globalisation both exacerbates existing forms of inequality and produces new forms in which some societies and groups become increasingly poorer and more vulnerable. This is most evident in the position and experience of disabled people. Globally, the vast majority of disabled people live in poverty, have no access to education and are disproportionately unemployed, underemployed and underpaid. In a thoughtful and important paper, Sheldon (2009) highlights some of the likely impacts of the current fiscal downturn on disability. The labour market and the vulnerability of disabled people in terms of both access to and continuance within work, as well as the increasing difficulties of external funding for user-led organisations and particular forms of critical and applied research, are some of the significant points of consideration. Raising the issue of disability studies in relation to this serious situation, the author gives particular emphasis to the urgent need for a shift towards political-economic thinking and the development of a 'global political economy of disability'. Engaging with these global dimensions should always act as a stimulus for recognising the importance of what we can learn from this process. This includes critically evaluating our own presuppositions, priorities and practices.

The question of voice

This important issue is connected to the politics of recognition, which concerns more than access or resource factors. Learning to speak for them-selves in an endeavour to increasingly seek to control choices and opportuni-ties in their lives, reinforces the centrality of the relationship between enhanced self-identity, understanding, solidarity and the pursuit of transforma-tive change. The focus of interest is multi-dimensional. It includes examining the context in which such voices are expressed; the content of these voices; and the purpose of such articulations and their impact on the change process.

Developing an informed knowledge and understanding of disability equal-ity issues raises many difficult questions and challenges, both personally and professionally. How we approach this engagement is part of a learning process. This has, and continues to raise, for me, such challenging questions as: What does it mean to listen to such voices? What can we learn from their ideas, insights and questions? What are the implications for the nature and purpose of sociological thinking and analysis? What challenges does the process of engagement raise for the relationship between, the disability community and more generally, civil society and the academy?

A question of research

Some of the most challenging and creative questions of disabled people have been in relation to the crucial issue of research. In 1986 with the support of Mike Oliver, a disabled scholar who has been a key influence in my life, the journal *Disability, Handicap and Society* (later called *Disability and Society*) was founded to provide a forum for the development of critical debate and analyses. The intention was to foreground the position and experiences of disabled people, foster dialogue and provide space that would encourage the development of new questions, insights, interpretations and alternative think-ing and practice with regard to research. This would include cross-cultural issues, insights and challenges (Barton 2009).

Mike Oliver and I organised a series of externally funded seminars during 1991 on the topic of 'Research'. The delegates included disabled scholars, activists and their allies. During these seminars, some of the most serious, critical, innovatory, exciting thinking and debate took place. It was a most creative process of learning. Several of the papers were submitted to the journal and published as a special issue on Researching Disability (*Disability, Handicap and Society* 1992, vol. 7, no. 2). These papers acted as a stimulus for an ongoing process of exploration over new ways of conceiving the purpose, process and outcomes of research.

These accounts were an attempt to begin to demystify research practice through documenting and examining the complex, contentious and contradictory nature of such work. A key emphasis was on what Oliver called 'the feasibility of a politics of the possible', which included 'a recognition of and a confrontation with power, which structures the social relations of research production' (1992, 110). This approach was in contrast to traditional forms of research in relation to disability. These papers raised the challenging and contentious question of the relevance of research, which encouraged an increasing explicit interest in questions of social justice, equity and citizenship based on a clear recognition that research was not to be viewed as disinterested or neutral. The question of change was also of significant importance, through the exploration and critique of discrimination and exclusion in its varied forms. Finally, the concern for informative, transformative research, which would contribute to alternative and enabling conceptions of disability, inclusive conditions and relations, was also of crucial importance. The contentiousness of these issues and their critical examination and re-examination, along with other related research concerns, have continued to be published in numerous papers within *Disability and Society* as well as the following examples: Clough and Barton (1995, 1998), Barnes and Mercer (1997), Walmsley and Johnson (2003) and Allan and Slee (2009).

This work, which is concerned with discussing issues beyond the field of disability studies, has raised a rich source of insights, understandings and questions. Two particular impacts that have been powerful in my own work have been the recognition that research can be disabling and harmful to the position and experience of marginalised and excluded groups. Also, it raises the immensely important question of our sense of audience as researchers and our responsibility to write in an accessible form. Nor must we underestimate the profound difficulties involved in developing more inclusive forms of thinking and research practice. There is still so much to learn and address on these issues.

In a recent publication based on the perspectives of 68 disabled people's organisations in 25 European countries, the findings clearly highlight the interest and eagerness to be involved in collaborative research by such organisations, but also raise some very serious concerns (Priestley, Waddington, and Bessozi 2010). These relate to the position of academic institutions over such research possibilities and the extent to which such an engagement will be based on equal partnership within social model and rights-based approaches to research. Several criticisms are made by the respondents based on their experiences of working with academic institutions. They also provide a range of topics that they believe new research needs to engage with. The degree of the challenges that such collaborative forms of emancipatory research raises, is expressed in the following way:

> Disabled people's organisations want to be equal partners in research projects. This is difficult. There are too many researchers who do not treat disabled people as equal partners. Disabled people want to help decide what kind of research is done. They want to get involved before the research starts. They want to help decide what questions to ask. They can help researchers to make their findings more accessible. Disabled people's organisations have good ideas for new research projects. (Priestley, Waddington, and Bessozi 2010)

The difference between laudable rhetoric and actual experience is often a serious issue within the research context. It should remind us of the importance of humility, the need for critical friendships and support, as well as the necessity of working hard at our knowledge and understanding of, and commitment to, the nature and purpose of research.

Conclusion

One of the benefits of developing a quality of respect for disabled people and their organisations is the degree to which they provide a fundamentally important knowledge and understanding of discrimination and exclusion. Another is the awareness that they demonstrate with regard to the recognition and critique of the very real difference that often exists between laudable rhetoric and claims over policy significance and the actual impact on their daily lives. Both of these factors provide a motivation for the pursuit of social justice, inclusive conditions and relations. They are also an essential antidote against the emerging trivialisation and simplification of these factors by those seeking quick, slick fixes, especially in programmes of professional preparation.

In encouraging a serious engagement with the voices of disabled people, I am not implying that this involves an uncritical stance of acceptance, or that their perspectives represent a homogenised set of ideas and understandings. What I am contending is that understanding inequality, and the processes that create and sustain it, is impossible without such insights. Indeed, 'research that lacks an insider-perspective, is at least one-dimensional and indeed, at worst, it is arrogant and misleading'.[1]

The urgency and necessity of the responsibility of listening to these voices can be understood when one appreciates historically how they have been viewed by political and professional gatekeepers to knowledge and opportunities within society. Firstly, at different points in history, they have been conceived as less than human, and therefore do not have the ability to fulfil this requirement. Hence, such expectations over their voices are ill-founded. Secondly, they are seen to have a voice, but it is viewed as inferior and thus they always need professionals and other personnel to speak for them. Both these approaches legitimate conceptions of pity and dependency on the part of disabled people. Finally, disabled people are recognised as having a voice, but it is dangerous, subversive, and needs to be regulated and silenced. For a transformative and emancipatory conception of voice, the views, interests and feelings of disabled people need to be at the centre of decision-making of both policy and practice relating to the quality of their lives. Micheline Mason, a disabled woman, highlights the importance of this issue in the following powerful statement:

> It is one of the most frustrating aspects of the lives of young people, disabled people, and people struggling with emotional distress that our own thinking is not sought when attempts are made to solve our problems. This is not to say we always know the answers, or that we never make mistakes, but that our perspective is often the 'missing piece' in the puzzle, the bit that reveals the whole picture. (Mason 2000, 116)

Thus, the question of voice involves engaging with issues of human rights, informed respect and active participatory citizenship.

A politics of hope, which is at the basis of their approach, is one that goes ultimately beyond the issue of disablement, to the struggle for a non-oppressive, non-discriminatory society for all. What I am advocating, is that through taking their voices seriously, we have much to learn from the experiential knowledge and understanding of disabled people.[2] This is a process that simultaneously can be disturbing, challenging and enriching in both the personal and professional aspects of our lives. It also raises profound questions about the culture and purpose of universities in relation to these fundamentally significant issues.

Notes
1. Private correspondence from Professor David Gillborn, Institute of Education, University of London.
2. To counter-balance an overly-romantic idealised conception of issues relating to disability studies, the disability movement and other important issues, see Oliver (2009).

References

Allan, J., and R. Slee. 2009. *Doing inclusive education research*. Rotterdam: Sense Publications.
Alur, M., and V. Timmons. 2009. *Inclusive education across cultures: Crossing boundaries, sharing ideas*. New Delhi: Sage Publications.
Armstrong, A.C., D. Armstrong, and I. Spandagou. 2010. *Inclusive education: International policy & practice*. London: Sage.
Barnes, C. 2003. Rehabilitation for disabled people: A 'sick' joke? www.leeds.ac.uk/disability-studies/archiveuk (accessed June 7, 2010).

Barnes, C., and G. Mercer, eds. 1997. *Doing disability research.* Leeds: Disability Press.

Barton, L. 2003. *Inclusive education and teacher education. A basis for hope or a discourse for delusion.* London: Institute of Education, University of London.

Barton, L. 2009. Transcript of audio interview Professor Len Barton. www.informaworld.com/smpp/educationarena interview online interview5-db=educ.

Barton, L., and F. Armstrong. 2000. Disability, education and inclusion: Cross-cultural issues and dilemmas. In *International handbook of disability studies,* ed. G. Albrecht, K. Seelman, and M. Bury. London: Sage Publications.

Clough, P., and L. Barton, eds. 1995. *Making difficulties: Research and the construction of SEN.* London: Paul Chapman.

Clough, P., and L. Barton, eds. 1998. *Articulating with difficulty: Research voices in inclusive education.* London: Paul Chapman.

Connell, R. 2007. *Southern theory: The global dynamics of knowledge in social science.* Sydney: Allen & Unwin.

Mason, M. 2000. *Incurably human.* Wembley: Adept Press.

Oliver, M. 1992. Changing the social relations of research production. *Disability, Handicap and Society* 7, no. 2: 101–14.

Oliver, M. 2009. *Understanding disability: From theory to practice.* 2nd ed. Basingstoke: Palgrave Macmillan.

Priestley, M., L. Waddington, and C. Bessozi. 2010. Towards an agenda for disability research in Europe: Learning from disabled people's organisations. *Disability and Society* 25, no. 6.

Sheldon, A. 2009. Recession, radicalism and the road to recovery? *Disability and Society* 24, no. 5: 667–71.

Walmsley, J., and K. Johnson. 2003. *Inclusive research with people with learning disabilities: Past, present and future.* London: Jessica Kingsley.

Len Barton

University of London, Institute of Education, UK

Index

Page numbers in **Bold** represent figures.

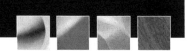

ROUTLEDGE

Related titles from Routledge

Disability Matters
Pedagogy, media and affect

Edited by Anna Hickey-Moody and Vicki Crowley

Disability Matters engages with the cultural politics of the body, exploring this fascinating and dynamic topic through the arts, teaching, research and varied encounters with 'disability' ranging from the very personal to the professional. Chapters in this collection are drawn from scholars responding in various registers and contexts to questions of disability, pedagogy, affect, sensation and education. Questions of embodiment, affect and disability are woven throughout these contributions, and the diverse ways in which these concepts appear emphasize both the utility of these ideas and the timeliness of their application.

This book was originally published as a special issue of *Discourse: Studies in the Cultural Politics of Education.*

December 2011: 246 x 174: 192pp
Hb: 978-0-415-69350-9
£80 / $125

Everyday Ethics
Reflections on Practice

Edited by Gretchen B. Rossman and Sharon F. Rallis

Everyday Ethics looks at the moments that demand moral consideration and ethical choice that arise as part of a researcher's daily practice. Drawing on principles of systematic inquiry as transparent and grounded in conceptual reasoning, it describes research as praxis and the researcher as practitioner. The researcher is a decision-maker for both procedural and ethical matters that attend the conduct of research, especially when the research is focused on human wellbeing. Every decision about data collection, analysis, interpretation, and presentation has moral dimensions. This book invites us to deepen our understanding of everyday ethics, and contributes to the ongoing discourse about research as moral practice, conducted by such reflexive practitioners.

This book was originally published as a special issue of the *International Journal of Qualitative Studies in Education*.

December 2011: 246 x 174: 136pp
Hb: 978-0-415-69341-7
£80 / $125

Family Support and Family Caregiving across Disabilities

Edited by George H.S. Singer, David E. Biegel and Patricia Conway

Family members provide the majority of care for individuals with disabilities in the United States. Recognition is growing that family caregiving deserves and may require societal support, and evidence-based practices have been established for reducing stress associated with caregiving. Despite the substantial research literature on family support that has developed, researchers, advocates and professionals have often worked in separate categorical domains such as family support for caregiving for the frail elderly, for individuals with mental illness, or for people with development disabilities.

This book addresses this significant limitation through cross-categorical and lifespan analyses of family support and family caregiving from the perspectives of theory and conceptual frameworks, empirical research and frameworks and recommendations for improvements in public policy. It also examines children with disabilities, children with autism, adults with schizophrenia, and individuals with cancer across the life cycle.

This book was published as a two-part special issue in the *Journal of Family Social Work*.

August 2011: 246 x 174: 216pp
Hb: 978-0-415-68268-8
£80 / $125